To Kevin + Karen

Lots
of
Love
From
Gemma

xxx
xxx
x
x

LINCOLNSHIRE

Edited by Carl Golder

First published in Great Britain in 2000 by
YOUNG WRITERS
Remus House,
Coltsfoot Drive,
Woodston,
Peterborough, PE2 9JX
Telephone (01733) 890066

HB ISBN 0 75432 008 1
SB ISBN 0 75432 009 X

FOREWORD

This year, the Young Writers' Up, Up & Away competition proudly presents a showcase of the best poetic talent from over 70,000 up-and-coming writers nationwide.

Successful in continuing our aim of promoting writing and creativity in children, our regional anthologies give a vivid insight into the thoughts, emotions and experiences of today's younger generation, displaying their inventive writing in its originality.

The thought, effort, imagination and hard work put into each poem impressed us all and again the task of editing proved challenging due to the quality of entries received, but was nevertheless enjoyable. We hope you are as pleased as we are with the final selection and that you continue to enjoy *Up, Up & Away Lincolnshire* for many years to come.

CONTENTS

Hannah Rose	69
Matthew Richardson	69
Ben Gardener	69
Emily Barber	70
Ashley Foulsham	70
Gemma Harrison	70
Nathan Guest	71
Laura Fung	71
Victoria Penta Cawthorn	72
Jade Wells	72
Danielle Sheanon	73
Amy Kettlewell	73
Bethan Hasnip	73
Laura Hudson	74
Laura Coates	74
Ben Thompson	75
Jack Hubbert	75
Jamie Tear	76
Felicity Maynard	76

St Andrew's CE Primary School, Leasingham

Cheryl Newton	76
Jemma Trollope	77
Amy Garwood	78
Simon Ross	78
Alannah Clelland	79
Elizabeth Crawford	80
Susannah McGagh	80
Liam Atkins	81
Rebecca Ramsden	82
Lisa Anderson	82
Clare Hedley-Smith	83
Mark Dowse	84
Christina Gould	84
Lee Stobart	85
Jessica Sargeant	85
Adam Woodmansey	86
Matthew Roope	86

Tom Richardson	87
Nicholas Hyde	87
David Martin	88
Gerry Flynn	88
Rachel Fisher	89
Alexander Watt	89
Charlotte Elkington	90
Jonathon Dunham	90
Ryan Callaghan-Jarvis	91
Matthew Turner	91
Laura Taylor	92
Elliot Brooke	92
Penny Cheung	93
Emily Brown	93

St Andrew's CE Primary School, Woodhall Spa

Steve Sharp	94
Pamela Rayward	95
Rebecca Lingard	96
Guy Coupland	96
Grace Finney	97
Harry Jackson	97
Chris Newstead	98
Simon Da Silva	98
Alex Smith	99
Sam Dearie	99
Belinda Pitwell	100
Jamie Rickell	100
Rachel Nelson	101
Chris Wright	101
James Ritson	102
Chris Jelly	102
Laura Cohu	103
Daniel Mehaffey	103
Daniel Gayton	104
Daniel Holland	104
Tom Walsh	105
Lee Creasey	105

St Augustine's Catholic Primary School, Stamford

Seathorne Primary School

Md Inamul Ahmed	125
Vicky Copley	126
Dale Amies	126
Connie Overton	127
Harry Clare	127
Joanna Kay Crooke	128
Laura Geaghan	128
Habibah Yasmin	129
Amy Willard	129
Jordan Cooper	130
Jessica Lindley	130
Adam Haywood	131
Jessegaron Verheul	131
Jeordie Ringsell	132
Todd Bangham	132
Jason O'Hara	132
Emma Bagnall	133
Vern Bee	133
Sarah Smith	133
Cassie Dreher	134
Laura Hamilton	135
Glenn Browne	136
Liam Topliss	137
Elliot Smith	137

Staniland Primary School

Robbie Mitchell	138
Rosa-Marie Woods	139
Sam Holland	140
Chanelle Swadling	141
Lesley Stones	142
Fiona Dukalskis	143
Karly Head	143
Sophie Stringer	144
Nathan Coupland	144
Emily Laura Jakeman	145
Hallam Williamson	146

Connor Young	183
Stacey Smalley	183
Jade Robinson	184
Kate Stratton	184
Sam Cooper	185
Arron Drew	185

Wrangle Primary School

Hannah Boyes	186
Becky Gostelow	186
Skye Cotter	187
Leon Bailey	187
George Kime	187
Rianna Hooke	188
Victoria Pinchbeck	188
Geoge Miller	189
Emma Garner	189
Daniel Bee	190
Chelsea Howes	190
James Arnold	191
Leigh Overton	191
Sarah Gostelow	192
Thomas Brooks	192
Charlotte Burton	193

Fleetwood Lane CP School

Jarron Marshall	193
Victoria Bray Whitworth	193
Jonathan Birchall	194
Jeremy Ely	194
Beth Davis	195
Stephanie Wilkinson	196
Daniel Godfrey	196
George Miller	197
Samuel Collins	197
Edward Ashton	198
Desmond Riley	198
Rishul Padhiar	199

The Poems

MY CAT GERALDINE

My cat Geraldine she sleeps all day,
My cat Geraldine rolls in the hay.
My cat Geraldine has only one eye,
My cat Geraldine eats chicken pie.

My cat Geraldine got very ill,
My cat Geraldine had to take a pill.
My cat Geraldine's hair fell out,
My cat Geraldine has not got gout.

My cat Geraldine met next door's cat,
My cat Geraldine is now rather fat.
My cat Geraldine met her fate
Under the wheels of a Rover estate.

James Nixon

CHRISTMAS

Christmas is a happy time,
Lots of food and lots of wine.
Christmas presents on the tree,
One for you and lots for me.

This one is a special date,
So let's make sure we celebrate,
With lots of laughter, lots of fun,
For this one is the millennium.

As we look forward to the twentieth century,
Think about the way the world is meant to be.
No wars, hunger, pain or tears,
But a peaceful world for the coming years.

Harry Pitcher (10)
Conway School

THE WORST SCHOOL

Every morning when the day is dawning,
I get up and go to school.
When we get to school the teacher is screaming,
But the boys are still dreaming.
We hand out the hymn books,
Rattling through the pages.
We looked at all the strange songs
That were wrote throughout the ages.

We walk quietly to assembly, pulling faces at the teacher,
The headmaster stands at the front, acting like a preacher.
Lunch is a major no-man's-land,
There's food bombs everywhere.
The waste bowl looks like someone's vomit
And there's mash potato on the chairs.
We think school will never end,
But at least we have a best friend.

Katherine Louise Larkin (10)
Conway School

DOLPHINS

Dolphins swim, dolphins glide
Dolphins jump, dolphins fly
Blue they are as blue as the sea
The sparkle in their eye makes you want to giggle
In the morning you look outside
A dolphin jumping makes you cry
To feed a dolphin is a treat
Their singing is so sweet.

Stephanie Clarke (10)
Conway School

MANCHESTER UNITED

M is for men
A is for ability
N is for Neville
C is for capability
H is for high scores
E is for ever winning
S is for skill
T is for *treble!*
E is for every title
R is for Ryan Giggs

U is for United
N is for natural
I is for Irwin
T is for teamwork
E is for ever
D is for *determination!*

Thomas Ruck (11)
Conway School

WORM

Whirling, curling
It moves up to the top of the ground
Looking out for birds in case it's their food round
As it flitters through the ground
It shakes from a thundering sound
Oh no, it's a bird I have been found
As it carries me up from the ground
I definitely know it's their food round!

Ben Herberts (11)
Conway School

STRANGE

There's a girl in my class
Who's very, very strange
Whenever she laughs
Her teeth shoot out at such a range

She eats caterpillars and slugs
She drinks mud from the ground
When we go out to play
She shouts, shouts, *shouts*

Sometimes she shrinks people
And vacuums them up
But sometimes she's OK I suppose
And she's my friend too.

Emma Kelly (10)
Conway School

MY BEST FRIEND

My best friend's an alien
She comes from outer space
She's got orange and pink skin
And a red and yellow face.

She likes to eat little boys
So that's why there's so few
You better be careful
Or she might be eating you.

I never leave my best friend's side
Me and her stick together
Me and my best friend
We'll be friends forever.

Holly Hague (9)
Conway School

MY HOUSE OF THE MILLENNIUM

My house of the millennium
Would be painted in thousands of colours,
Yellow, orange, pink and green,
Purple, red, turquoise and blue.

My house of the millennium
Would be built where everyone could see it,
It would be big and tall,
Very pretty and cool,
It would be funky and groovy and all.

My house of the millennium
Would be exactly what I had wished for,
Nobody would want anything more,
It would have to be a dream come true,
I would have servants and maids and everything,
There wouldn't be a thing I would have to do.

Cara Grantham (10)
Conway School

MY PET

One day I took my pet alligator to school,
He went human fishing in the swimming pool.
I was going to take him off the lead,
But the teacher disagreed.
Then secretly I let him loose
And he was acting like a crazy moose.
He dived into the pool,
Where it was nice and cool.
At home time he bit the headmaster's ear
And all the mothers fainted just about *here*.

Alexandra Spalding (11)
Conway School

WE ANIMALS SET ASTRAY

I am a cat set astray,
I get beaten up by dogs all day,
I wish I had a home with lots of rats,
It would be nice to have a mat.

I am a dog with fleas,
I struggle and I strain,
If only someone would take me in,
They call me dumb, if only they knew how it felt.

I am a mouse so small,
They try to eat me up,
If only someone would care,
I wish there was someone with whom I could share
The cosiness of their home.

Abhishek Nayak (9)
Conway School

MY TEDDY

I've had my teddy all my life
So I know everything about him
I call him Caca since it's the first thing I said
Only I know he's afraid of ephlumps and wouvel
(elephants and weasels)
And seeing he's a black monkey he loves to go to the zoo
Especially Woburn Safari Park
Of course his favourite bit is the monkey drive through
But when he gets to see the ephlumps and wouvels
He goes crazy.

Joe Grant (10)
Conway School

IN THE 25TH CENTURY

The place where I am now,
How I got here I don't know how.
A red surface lies at my feet,
Some people say 'It's pretty neat!'

I see a spaceship zooming past,
Two hundred and fifty miles per hour,
To you on Earth that very fast,
But to us you couldn't go slower!

I live in a house of metal
On a place you've never been to,
I've been there since I was little,
Maybe one day you can come too.

I visited Neptune a while back,
The eighth planet from the sun.
On the way back we had a problem
And I tell you that was no fun.

So if you ever get a chance
To see this place in the stars,
Spaceships travel the speed of light,
To an inhabited planet named Mars.

Matthew Wilson (11)
Conway School

A SUMMER POEM

I wish summer would come again
Summer brings me happiness
When summer goes I'm sad again
Until it's time for summer again.

Adam Berry (9)
Conway School

SEASONS OF THE YEAR

Spring is coming,
Spring is near,
Spring is great fun,
Spring is here.

Winter has gone,
Winter isn't near,
Guess what winter brings?
Winter brings Christmas cheer.

Summer is hot,
Sometimes summer is wet,
Guess what my sisters do?
They're playing with my pet.

Laura Presgrave (9)
Conway School

I WISH THAT I COULD FLY

I wish that I could fly,
High into the sky,
Whenever I left they would say goodbye,
I wish that I could fly.

I wish that I could fly,
Before your very eyes,
To fly I think I'd die,
I wish that I could fly.

I wish that I could fly,
It is not a lie,
Become a wonder of the sky,
I wish that I could fly.

Richard Glenn (10)
Conway School

DOGS AND MYSELF

Dogs are cute and cuddly,
Opening your heart,
Growling, barking, whining too,
So much fun and smart.

And when it is lunch time,
Nothing stops me
Dumping food under the table for my doggie.

My dog is the best one,
Yes I'm sure,
So, so smart,
Even opening the door,
Loving, caring, funny too,
I say to my doggie 'I love you.'

Harriet Tunnard (9)
Conway School

I AM A CAT

I am a cat
And I keep away from cold
I am loved dearly because I am like gold
I always lick my paws and never moan or cry
And when I am not given my food I feel I am going to die.

I am a cat
And I try to catch mice
And when I have caught them they taste very nice
When I come in and go to sleep
Then until morning I never take a peep.

Sophie Grant (10)
Conway School

I WISH . . .

I wish,
> That I could fly,
>> I'd fly to Brazil to watch the football,
>> I'd fly to Spain to swim in the sea,
>> I'd fly to Chesterfield to see my second cousins
>> And I'd fly to India and be reincarnated as a bee.

I wish,
> That I could fight monsters,
>> I'd fight the monster below my bed,
>> I'd fight the monster that lives in me,
>> ` I'd fight the monster that lives in the sea
>> And I'd fight the monster who hangs overhead.

I wish,
> That I could live in a tent,
>> Live free all day
>> And pay no rent,
>> Oh I wish I could live in a tent.

> If I could do any of these, life would be bliss.

Elizabeth Dawes (10)
Conway School

THINKING OF A POEM

I wish I could think of a poem
They're really hard to do
But when you get one started
Then you whiz right through
This one's a short one
Because I can't think of much
I wish I could think of a poem
They're really hard to do.

I wish I could think of a poem
They're really hard to do
But when you get one started
Then you whiz right through
I've done a second verse
Because one's not long enough
I wish I could think of a poem
They're really hard to do!

Sophie Hardy (10)
Conway School

JOOSTER

My name is Jooster
I am a rabbit
A very playful rabbit
I have two friends
Their names are Tiger and Patch
We eat, eat and eat.

My favourite food is crisps
Patch's is vegetables
Tiger's is cookies
We all run around a lot
When my owner comes we run.

I am a very unusual rabbit
I talk to my friends and
My owner
Now it is time to go to bed
Goodnight.

Natalie Goodall (9)
Conway School

FRIENDS

Be good, be kind
Let's make the bad things unwind
Be cool, be great
There is nobody who I hate.

Christmas is a lovely time of year
It's fun, it's great for friends - that's just begun
The sparkle in your eyes tells me you agree
I know we are going to be great friends
You and me.

Come to my house for a sleepover
In the deep, dark night we will grab a bite
Then we will ascend up to bed
And rest our head.

Charlotte Thompson (9)
Conway School

A FARMER

I wish I was a farmer
A farmer I could be.

I could cut the corn
And check the beet
A farmer I could be.

I could build a shed
And a house
A farmer I could be.

I could drive a lorry
Drive a tractor
A farmer I'm going to be.

George Hoyes (9)
Conway School

I WANT

I want to go under the sea
And swim with all the fish.
I want to go out clubbing,
And stay up all the night.

I want to have a party
And do whatever I want.
I want to be free
And fly like a bird.

I feel really cool,
To do what I want.

Julia Kinder (10)
Conway School

COLOURS OF AUTUMN

Leaves falling from the trees
All different colours
Yellow like sand, orange like honey
Red ones are like lipstick and brown like mud
Toddlers playing in the leaves
Soon it will be Hallowe'en
When children get dressed up
Night-time - a strong wind
Leaves zooming, whirling, shooting!
All night long
Morning is here
And we're playing in the leaves
Autumn is great!

Gemma Craig (9)
Cranwell Primary School

THE CHURCH

I step into the church,
A musty smell wafts past my nose.
I see some people kneeling by a pew
And a vicar saying a prayer.
I see a man at the back,
Bowing his head begging for forgiveness
And a man washing his face
Driving the evil spirits away.
I take some holy water,
As soon as the cold water touches my face,
I feel like 1,000 knives are stabbing into me,
But in my heart I feel it has done me good.
I talk to the vicar,
He has a gentle voice.
I bow my head and speak to God,
He forgives me.

Robbie McCrea (10)
Cranwell Primary School

THE CHURCH

I walked into the church,
the old smell hit me,
it was lovely and warm,
but the benches were hard
and they were cold.
As I walked around
the vicar turned off the lights
and it all went cold,
but God will always
keep me warm.

Guy Davies (10)
Cranwell Primary School

MY FEELINGS

The small, old church shadowed over me,
As I walked into the building.
The light was gloomy and dim,
The smell dusty and musty,
The pews were smooth yet rough
And the cold wrapped its fingers around me.

I wandered around,
Not lost, but in thought
And stared at the beautiful stained glass windows.
Sometimes I wonder what they mean,
Maybe God means more.

Daniel Sainsbury (11)
Cranwell Primary School

DO YOU LIKE THE SOUND OF . . .

Lorries roaring down the motorway,
Trees breaking in the wind,
Golf balls smashing through windows,
Glass shattering in a car crash,
Sirens blaring on the fire engine,
Babies crying for their milk,
Children splashing in the swimming pool,
Churches collapsing in the earthquake,
Cars spinning to a halt,
Swings screeching back and forth?

Thomas Duerden (10)
Gedney Church End School

THIS IS JUST TO SAY . . .

I have taken your eggs
that came from the farmhouse

And you most probably
wanted to hatch them.

Sorry for taking them, they
were just right and tasted
delicious!

Jacqueline Russell (11)
Gedney Church End School

CHRISTMAS EVE

Santa Claus is cold,
Children are building snowmen,
Reindeer are eating their carrots.

Snow is on the floor,
Scrumptious puds being eaten,
Santa is on his way.

Nicola Clayton (10)
Gedney Church End School

WILD

A parrot in its nest
is like a log on a river.
A panther in his tree
is like a stone in the air.
A lizard sunbathing in his tree
is like a boat on the sea.

Luke Goatcher (10)
Gedney Church End School

THE SUN

Day shiner,
Bright whirler,
Day spinner,
Yellow winder,
Reflect shiner,
Heat giver,
Fire heater,
Eye catcher,
Sky breaker.

Craig Bailey (9)
Gedney Church End School

SIMILE

A dormouse in its nest,
Like a pebble in a bed of leaves.

A bird gliding through the sky,
Like an aeroplane soaring through the clouds.

A dog in its kennel asleep,
Like a walnut in its shell.

Grace Rankin (10)
Gedney Church End School

A WINTER'S MORNING

In the window sill
We see the big snowman there,
With shimmering clouds.

Stefan Fox (10)
Gedney Church End School

WINTER TIMES

People sledge in the snow
And people like the winter
And they play fun games.

People sledge in the snow.
They throw snow at each other
And it is good fun.

People sledge in the snow.
They throw snow at each other,
Like best friends playing.

Charles Heasman (11)
Gedney Church End School

SIMILE

A dormouse in its nest,
Like a pebble in a bed of leaves.

A bird gliding through the sky,
Like an aeroplane soaring through the clouds.

A dog in its kennel asleep,
Like a walnut in its shell.

Andrew Still (9)
Gedney Church End School

WINTER DAYS

Winter's very cold,
It's silent after the snow.
The snow makes footprints.

Kelly Shaw (11)
Gedney Church End School

WINTER WONDERS

A white Christmas comes,
Icy with white winter snow,
Warmth has gone, I know.

Glittering frost comes,
Winter snowmen that we make,
Bring joy to children.

Eve Martyn (10)
Gedney Church End School

ANIMAL SIMILES

A cheetah running on the plains,
Like a Mercedes CLK on the road.

A bat sucking blood,
Like a snail's trail.

A baby whale splashing in the sea,
Like a human in the swimming pool.

Jonathon Congreve (9)
Gedney Church End School

THE BEAST OF 2000

The beast of 2000 only comes every thousand years,
It comes out at night when we are celebrating.
Aaaaargh! Here he comes, steaming up the stairs,
So two more words - goodbye now!

Samuel Taylor (9)
Heckington St Andrew CE School

THE SHIPWRECK

A desolate island,
Surrounded by miles of ocean and sea,
A ship sails by, heading for the rocks,
A man watching in silent despair.

He made no effort to help.
Just stood there, his head hung down with guilt,
Thunder clashed, as the storm blew the ship towards the rocks,
Like cat to a mouse.

In the tempest the man lost sight of them,
He heard the splinters of wood cracking,
Then all was silent.

As the mist glided away,
The man flew down to the shore.
Would she be there?
Would she be alive?

His heart leapt,
He gazed into her sad blue eyes as they flickered,
She was alive.
Then she woke up complete,
She started to walk off arm-in-arm with her
Long-lost father, together at last.

Jennifer Cutting (9)
Heckington St Andrew CE School

THE LOST AND GONE CHEESECAKE

You were my only friend, now you are gone.
How can I live without you?
My life is coming to an end without you.
You were the most wonderful cheesecake
I have ever seen and tasted.

I cannot sleep without you;
All my dreams are bad without you.
I have cried so much there are no tears left.
You cheered me up when I was sad,
Now I am absolutely devastated without you.

Anna Keeping (10)
Heckington St Andrew CE School

TO SPOT A WITCH

To spot a witch
You must notice a twitch
That they do when they smell you around.
If their eyes bright green glow
You instinctively know
That you had best move your immediate ground.

The only way
So the witch wastes away
Is to point at them,
Glare at them,
Make them feel bad.
And if that doesn't work, do the opposite.

You must next to them sit.
You must hug them
And kiss them
And make them feel at home.
You'll change their feelings,
Confuse them a lot,
Destroy their home plot.

They'll shout 'Not that!'
Deflate, and go *splat!*

Rebecca Such (10)
Heckington St Andrew CE School

DOGS AND CATS

Dogs are fun and so are we,
Cats do tricks and so do we,
Dogs do everything, so do you and me,
Cats look sad and so do we,
Dogs look around and so do you and me,
Some cats are big, some cats are small,
Some like eating fish,
Dogs jump and so do you and me,
Cats are cuddly and so are you and me,
Dogs are fast and so are we,
Cats are lovely and so are you,
Dogs are big, some are small, just like me.

Megan Davy (10)
Heckington St Andrew CE School

MY BEAR

I have a bear, a very brown bear
who has no hair, but fur!
He does not purr or roar or bark,
but he does growl!
He has no fingers, he has no toes
but he does have paws and claws
and very sharp teeth!
He's not very vicious,
he's really quite sweet!
I think he's the best!

Emily McMath (9)
Heckington St Andrew CE School

THE LOST AND GONE ICE-CREAM SUNDAE

Oh sundae, oh sundae, I need my ice-cream sundae!
With your beautiful, yummy, tasty chocolate sauce!
And your lovely vanilla ice-cream, your wonderfully
whipped vanilla ice-cream. Why did you leave me?
Why did you leave me? Where you used to sit in the kitchen
is now bare and cold looking. Why did you leave me?
Why did you leave me? We were so happy together!
You used to sit on my pillow and we would sing ourselves to sleep.
Why did Aunty have to eat you? She ruined our lives!
Oh sundae, you were so beautiful, when I was sad
you would cheer me up. I miss you so much!
I cannot live without you! Goodbye!

Jessica Powell (9)
Heckington St Andrew CE School

THE LOST AND GONE CHEESECAKE

He was a good cheesecake, he served his country
and his fellowship people.
How can I live for the rest of my life without my cheesecake?
You were always there when I needed you,
the only things left are the crumbs and the
big, empty space on my plate.
Poor cheesecake, it was so lovely and wonderful
but now it's gone. It was so wonderful
I could taste it in my mouth.

Robert Barr (9)
Heckington St Andrew CE School

SHAPES

Triangles, triangles and rectangles,
Squares and circles and octagons.
I say I love shapes, and I mean,
I love shapes.
Shapes, shapes are great.

Hannah Burton (8)
Heckington St Andrew CE School

THUNDER AND LIGHTNING

Light shining bright
Through the night,
What a bright night,
What a scary sight!

Bang, bang, bang,
Flash, flash, flash,
Cars all go splash, splash, splash.

Dark stormy clouds
People in houses,
Soaking wet coats,
Scares the goats.

Drab, steely sky,
Umbrellas held high,
Rain becomes drops,
Slows and stops,
Doors open wide,
People step outside.

Charlotte Powers (7) & Phoebe Haller (6)
Kirkby On Bain Primary School

WHAT IS THE MOON?

The moon is a clock without the hands.
It is a quarter of an apple without the pips.
The moon is a plate without the pattern.
It is a slice of cheese without the holes.
The moon is a chocolate orange without the tap.
It is an alarm without the ring.
The moon is a ring without the diamonds.
It is a cake dish without the gold.
The moon is the sun without the warmth.
It is a bin lid without the rubbish.
The moon is a glass without the water.
It is a tyre without the tread.
The moon is a golf ball without the writing.
It is a football without the kick.
The moon is the Millennium Wheel without the glass rooms.
It is a rose without the petals.
The moon is a cake without a cherry.
It is a balloon without its basket.
The moon is a roll of sellotape without the tape.
It is a pin without the spike.
The moon is a beach ball without the colours.
It is a jam jar without the jar.
The moon is a star without the shine.
It is a dog bowl without the food.
The moon is the end of a party popper without the confetti.
It is a banana without the skin.
The moon is a hair band without the colour.
It is a boomerang without the spin.
The moon is a 'C' without a sound.
It is a smile without the lipstick.
The moon is the Millennium Dome without the spikes.
It is a face without eyes, nose and mouth.
The moon is a milk bottle top without the milk.

Class 2 (6 - 9 years)
Kirkby On Bain Primary School

SUNSHINE

Sunny
  days
    come
      bright
      shiny
        sun
          making
           plants
             grow
               sparkling
               rivers
                 glow.

Living
  on
    holiday
      friends
        to
          stay
           play
             on
               the
                 sand
                   tractors
                     plough
                   land

Light
  glittery
   sunset
    children
     in
      bed
       here
        is
          night
           streetlamps
            make
             light.

Daniel Haresign & Emily Colley (8)
Kirkby On Bain Primary School

SUN

Sun in the sky
Way up high.

Birds sing songs
Days are long.

Big ball of fire
Nine times higher.

Trees sparkle bright
In the sun's light.

Sun is yellow,
Cows in the meadow.

The sun goes down,
Moon goes to town.

Alex Lawson (7) & Andrew Chapman (6)
Kirkby On Bain Primary School

SNOW

When it is snowing
the snow is glowing
and the stars are flowing
all
    day
        long.

Snowflakes are spinning
pinning on the ground
making a funny sound
on
    the
        crowd.

When the children go outside
they stay and
play
    all
        day.

When it is night the
snow
    is
        bright.

Reed Allen, Ryan Grave (8) & Barry Holden (10)
Kirkby On Bain Primary School

RAIN

Spitting, splashing rain,
Grey, metal drain.
Puddles down street,
Cold wet feet.

Black sparkling sky,
Birds fly high,
'I want out'
Harassed rain shouts.

Bethany Lacey (7)
Kirkby On Bain Primary School

WEATHER

Sun shines
High
Up in the
Sky
Tweeting
Birds
Sing
Loud
Bells
Ring
Trees Grow
Up
Play
With
My Pup
Traffic
Lights
On
The
Street
I
Meet.

Callum Lockyear & Rupert Clark (6)
Kirkby On Bain Primary School

RAIN

Rain
  Dripping
    Down
      To
        The
          Ground
            Plop
              Plop
                Plop
                  It
                    Hits
                      The
                        Ground
                          Wet
                            Window
                              Drips
                                Looks
                                  Like
                                    Pips
                                      Full
                                        Gushing
                                          Gutter
                                            Spit
                                              Spat
                                                Splutter.

George Thompson (7) & Andrew Avison (6)
Kirkby On Bain Primary School

SUNNY DAYS

Blazing
Hot
Day
Warm
Sun
In May
Sunbathing
Mums
Lie
Blue
Bright
Sky.

Sun
Is
Still
Shining
When
The
Birds
Are
Flying.

The
Bees
Are
Buzzing
Into
The Honey
Homes.

Louisa Hoyes & Samantha Clayton (8)
Kirkby On Bain Primary School

SNOW

I
  like
    snow
      makes
        fingers
         glow
           small
             flowers
              die
                birds
                  don't
                    fly.

Slippery
  slidey
    sledge
      watch
      out
        hedge
          whizz
            bang
              bash
              oh
                dear
                  crash.

Children
  like
    snow
      run
        and
          throw
            hit
              and
                hurt
                  clean
                    the dirt.

Edward Parkinson & Richard Dulake (7)
Kirkby On Bain Primary School

UP ABOVE

Up into the highest tree I climb,
Reaching up to the sturdiest branches,
Struggling through tumbling leaves,
Finally reaching the top from where I can see.

Tall skyscrapers reaching up to the heavens.
Tiny people weaving in and out of buildings,
Cars zooming through the big city like flies
Skipping from leaf to leaf,
Aeroplanes roaring through the air
Leaving a trail of white smoke behind them,
Fields of golden corn waving gently in the breeze,
Combines waiting eagerly in their sheds for harvest time.
Snowy mountains showing off their jagged peaks,
Ice glistening in the bright sunlight.
The cool blue sea rippling towards distant shores.

Thomas Wilkinson (9)
Long Sutton Primary School

UP ABOVE

Up into the highest tree I climb,
Reaching up to the sturdiest branches,
Struggling through the tumbling leaves,
Finally reaching the top from where I can see.

Rose bushes that look like dots,
The further they go, the smaller they become,
Forest hedgehogs scurrying home to their leafy nests,
Their prickles sharp as thorns.
Blue tits being spied on by impatient cats,
Yorkshire terriers barking noisily,
Ponds full of glimmering, golden fish,
Black tadpoles slowly swimming round,
Sandy beaches with people bathing,
Delicate shells being covered by the dark green sea,
Rows of terraced houses, happy children playing
                        in the small gardens,
A man's keys being carried away by a black and
                               white magpie.

Lauren English (9)
Long Sutton Primary School

WINTER

W ild whistle, falling down,
I   ce makes the freezing ponds twinkle,
N ow the icicles hanging from the caves,
T   rees with silver sparkle
E verything is frozen and sparkling
R obins sing in the wind.

Matthew Smith (7)
Long Sutton Primary School

UP ABOVE

Up into the highest tree I climb,
Reaching up to the sturdiest branches,
Struggling through the tumbling leaves,
Finally reaching the top from where I can see -

Black smoke coiling from factory chimneys,
Reaching up to the blue sky,
Birds soaring swiftly through the heavens,
Their irritated predator, the cat, watching from far below,
Tiny human ants scuttling around,
Disappearing into houses and quickly popping out again,
Rivers trickling along and then opening out into vast lakes
Where small crafts race up and down,
The sun hanging in the sky like a golden ball,
Its shining beams pounding down on the Earth,
White clouds looking like legendary dragons,
With smoke escaping from their nostrils,
A colourful rainbow reaching across the sky
Touching the blessed borders of Dreamland,
Snow-capped mountains adorned with beautiful flowers,
Red, blue, yellow and orange.

Samuel Bradley (9)
Long Sutton Primary School

WINTER

W ild snowflakes twirl down
I cy trees shiver with tingly icicles like fingers
N ow trees sparkle like glittering stars
T winkling icicles fall from the trees
E very bit of snow comes to life
R obins sing in the wind, it feels like magic.

Zoe Brown (7)
Long Sutton Primary School

ICE-CREAM

Ice-cream melts quickly, lick it
before it drips. Yum, yum, my
mouth is cold.   My flake is
lovely, nice   and chocolatey.
My teeth   are feezing.
Drip, drop,   drip, drop.
Quickly,   lick it!
Yum, yum, yum,
good   I like
ice - cream.
I   like
ice-cream
especially
strawberry
flavour.
It is
sure
g
o
o
d

Susan Piccaver (7) & Eleanor Rayment (7)
Long Sutton Primary School

WINTERTIME

When it is cold
The big fat giant comes out with his stick.
He knocks the snowflakes down off the trees.
It makes the ground all clean and white.

Jack Tilbrook (6)
Long Sutton Primary School

Up Above

Up into the highest tree I climb,
Reaching up to the sturdiest branches,
Struggling through the tumbling leaves,
Finally reaching the top from where I can see -

The sun like a red fireball
Blazing down on the Earth,
I gaze into a clear, blue sky,
White clouds floating in the breeze,
I see brightly coloured sailing boats
Bobbing about on the water,
The sea, shining like diamonds scattered on its waves,
A ginger cat lazing in a garden,
Watching the pigeons go by,
Night-time stars like sequins,
A smooth river, ducks swimming amongst the ripples,
A glittering rainbow over my head,
As I sit perched in the top of the tree.

Joseph Ward (9)
Long Sutton Primary School

Winter

W ild icy pond talking to itself
I   ce twinkling down in the glowing night
N ice snowmen gliding in the sky
T ime to make the magic begin
E verything's invisible
R obins sing like flying snowflakes.

Rebecca Santry (7)
Long Sutton Primary School

UP ABOVE

Up into the highest tree I climb,
Reaching up to the sturdiest branches,
Struggling through the tumbling leaves,
Finally reaching the top from where I can see -

Blue waves on the rough sea
washing up on the shell-covered sand,
A dark, gloomy castle
surrounded by a moat,
Black and white seagulls
hovering like a spinning, cold tornado,
An old, grey church
ringing its noisy bells,
Crazy aeroplanes zooming quickly in and out of white,
fluffy clouds,
Beeping traffic in a line, angry people waiting
impatiently,
Fiercesome cats chasing loveable birds through
the green parks,
Tiny children playing with exciting tops.

Simon Fell (9)
Long Sutton Primary School

WINTER

W hite the snow floats in the air.
I cicles dripping in the freezing night.
N ight shivers with icicles dripping off window sills.
T he shivering birds in the snow.
E veryone makes a snowman.
R obins sing during the day.

Louise Thompson (7)
Long Sutton Primary School

UP ABOVE

Up into the highest tree I climb,
Reaching up to the sturdiest branches,
Struggling through the tumbling leaves,
Finally reaching the top from where I
can see -

Boats full of freshly-caught fish,
The postman doing early morning rounds,
Everyone just waking up from a
good night's sleep,
Factories opening as the sun rises,
Birds twittering and bees buzzing as they
fly through the light blue sky,
Green leaves lying on the ground rustling
as the wind gently blows,
A cat resting on the wet, dew-covered grass,
Flowers dancing in extraordinary gardens.

Machaela Smith (9)
Long Sutton Primary School

AUTUMN OUTSIDE

Autumn outside
Cobwebs are sparkling
Sparkling with dew
Some looking pretty
And some not at all
Trees looking ugly
Without any leaves
Branches are brown
Some rotting away.

Ashley Hefford (10)
Long Sutton Primary School

UP ABOVE

Up into the highest tree I climb,
Reaching up to the sturdiest branches,
Struggling through the tumbling leaves,
Finally reaching the top from where I can see -

The sea bumping up and down,
I see lighthouses come on, off,
A purring cat just waking up,
Some little ants just went home.

I see a rainbow crossing a bridge,
The sea washing the delicate shells,
A sunset starting to go down,
Sailing boats ready to sail across the sea.

I look down on the ground and see some beetles,
A nest full of speckled eggs,
They start to crack open,
Little chicks chirruping for food.

Rivers floating by, fish swimming around,
People walking into town,
The insects jumping in long grass
I see burning sun among the breeze.

Lauren Bloy (8)
Long Sutton Primary School

HAIKU

In the dark blue sky
The flashes of lightning shine
While thunder rumbles.

Katie Blackbourne (11)
Long Sutton Primary School

COLOUR

What is green? Green is like a lush green
tree swaying in the wind.
What is blue? Blue is like the rain dripping
down the shabby drainpipes.
What is pink? Pink is like a rose in a wonderful
garden shining in the moonlight.
What is gold? Gold is like a door handle
twinkling in the light.
What is purple? Purple is like a colouring
crayon being scribbled in a book.
What is silver? Silver is like glitter on
someone's work.
What is yellow? Yellow is like a great
pyramid in Egypt.
What is black? Black is like a necklace
shining on your neck.
What is orange? Orange is like a juicy
orange that you eat.
What is white? White is like a swan in
tropical blue water.
Now you know the wonderful colours of the world!

Ester Busley (8)
Long Sutton Primary School

A WINTER TREE

The branches look like ice
Frosty and silvery.
The tree's dying.
The icicles fall off the branches.
The snow falls too.

Charlie Wing (6)
Long Sutton Primary School

WINTER

W hite snow comes floating down.
I   cy ponds shine in the night.
N ow the frozen kids are still.
T   he sparkling icicles hang from the trees.
E   verything is still in its place.
R   obins glide through the sky to hunt for food.

Sophie Wetherall (7)
Long Sutton Primary School

WINTER

W hite snowflakes come floating down like a ball falling.
I   ce is twinkling like a scary ghost.
N ow the old wise trees are dead, with no life.
T   he little plants cannot grow.
E   verything is shining in the moonlight
R   obins are like big fat balls.

Victoria Navarrete (7)
Long Sutton Primary School

WINTER

Winter creeps in the silent forest
Fields are full with snow
Ducks slip on the icy ponds
Snow dies down
And falls on the ground
Then turns into freezing water
Everything turns white.

Matthew Bull (9)
Long Sutton Primary School

WINTER

W hite winter shows its face
I ce freezes quickly
N othing can stop the winter overtaking
T hrough the night everything stands still
E verything is frozen stiff.
R obins' voices flow in the wind.

Maxwell Burrell (7)
Long Sutton Primary School

ICICLES

I ce is cold in winter.
C old snowflakes on the ground.
I am cold in winter.
C old snow to make snowmen.
L etters coming saying 'Merry Christmas.'
E veryone is inside.
S nowmen staring at me.

James Heywood (7)
Long Sutton Primary School

SNOWY DAYS

I like snowy days
Glittering and beautiful snow
Snow is cold and I shiver
And I wear my hat and gloves
I like it in the snow
I play hide and seek and
Bradley and Joshua play with me.

Sophie Davis (6)
Long Sutton Primary School

COLOURS!

What is blue? Sparkling water is blue,
flowing down the fountain.

What is red? A rose is red,
with its velvet petals opening.

What is orange? A pumpkin is orange,
spooking people at Hallowe'en.

What is yellow? Sand is yellow,
at the sunny beach waiting for you.

What is grey? Dolphins are grey,
jumping high and low in the water.

Now you know how colourful
the world really is.

Zara Wakefield (8)
Long Sutton Primary School

A PERSON

A runner
A biker
A sleeper
An eater
A walker
A talker
A book reader
A thinker
A daydreamer
A child-keeper
What is this?

Sadie Carnell (10)
Long Sutton Primary School

WHAT ARE COLOURS?

What is orange? Orange is the gleaming
sun, shining in the sky.
What is yellow? Yellow is a bright
melon growing on a tropical tree.
What is blue? Blue is the bright
blue cloudy sky above us.
What is green? Green is the exotic
leaves, swaying on a palm tree.
What is red? Red is juicy strawberries
growing in the summer sun.
What is silver? Silver is the twinkling
moon, glimpsing down at us.
What is black? Black is the midnight
sky, with its gloomy dark background.
These are the colours that exist
in our beautiful world!

Elysha Summerfield (8)
Long Sutton Primary School

FROST

The frost is freezing and cold.
Winter is coming, my hands are cold.
Snowflakes are tumbling to the ground.
Wear your hats and gloves and even scarves.
Glittery fast snow comes to the ground.
Soft wind is blowing.
The frost is cold.
Leaves are falling to the snowy ground.
In the morning frost is on my window
When I am outside I put my big coat on.

George Robson (7)
Long Sutton Primary School

COLOURS OF THE WORLD

What is green? Green is like tree leaves
swaying in the autumn breeze.
What is red? A poppy is red
in its winter sleep.
What is silver? A penny is silver
shining in the till.
What is pink? A rose is pink
waving in the summer garden.
What is violet? Violet is the sun
setting in the coloured sky.
What is black? Black is like the shadow
of a haunted ghost.
What is brown? Brown is like hot melting chocolate
in the blazing sun.
What is gold? Gold is like the corn
swaying in the summer breeze.
Now isn't there loads of colours in the world?

Zoe Wright (9)
Long Sutton Primary School

THE WINTER WIND

The winter is cold and bitter.
The cold snow is falling down.
Warm hats and gloves, scarves as well.
The snow is like a glittering carpet.
Scary trees are bare and brown.
There's not a sound from anything
Apart from the whistling wind.
Cold snowflakes falling down from the dark sky.
I play in the snow all day long.

Katherine Anderson (7)
Long Sutton Primary School

WHAT IS RED?

What is red? Your face turns red
When you're laughing out loud.
What is blue? The sky is blue
Where birds are hovering around.
What is purple? A grape is purple
With its juicy insides.
What is yellow? The desert is yellow
With its horrible sandstorms.
What is orange? A tiger is orange
With its sharp, devouring teeth.
What is green? The grass is green
With its lush, green blades.
What is gold? A goldfish is gold
With its tail swishing in the deep blue lake.
What is silver? A coin is silver
Being spent nearly every day.
These are some of the colours of the world.

Thomas Bradford (9)
Long Sutton Primary School

WINTER TREES

Trees shivering in the sky
Covered in the frost.
Trees losing leaves
Trees all sparkly
Covered in glittering snow.
Icicles hanging from trees.
Snowy trees by the roadside.
Silvery snow sparkling,
Sparkling as it comes down.

Thomas Day (6)
Long Sutton Primary School

UP ABOVE

Up into the highest tree I climb,
Reaching up to the sturdiest branches,
Struggling through the tumbling leaves,
Finally reaching the top from where I can see -

Army ants building their delicate nest,
Ready to nip anyone who tries to destroy it,
Fish swimming through the tropical waves,
Mysterious birds hovering patiently amongst the clouds,
Sheep in lonely fields, snuggling up to keep warm,
Angry seas bashing against sleeping rocks,
Children playing amongst trapped trees,
Glittering rays of golden beams coming from the blazing sun,
A rainbow of colour like a bridge of dreams.

Joseph Abram (9)
Long Sutton Primary School

SNOWFLAKES

S   nowflakes falling down, down, down
N   ow the people are making snowmen
O   h I said to my friends, look at that
      glittering snowflake
W   e all like making snowmen
F   alling snowflakes on the ground
L   ooking for leaves on the floor
A   snowball fight . . . *come on*
K   icking the snow around
E   veryone is having fun
S   nowflakes falling down, down, down.

Zoe Wells (7)
Long Sutton Primary School

UP ABOVE

Up into the highest tree I climb,
Reaching up to the sturdiest branches,
Struggling through the tumbling leaves,
Finally reaching the top from where I can see -

A beautiful rainbow arching like a bridge over a river,
A magnificent butterfly with giant wings
                    landing on a rotten branch,
The sun setting in the darkening heavens,
People down below scurrying about like tiny ants,
A gentle breeze rippling the sparkling river,
A distant field filled with dancing flowers,
Sparkling green grass covered in tiny drops of dew,
Cars crawling along like ebony black beetles.

Laura Bell (9)
Long Sutton Primary School

WINTER SUNSET

The winter tree is cold
Silver frost that is freezing
Tree in the sunset
Tree glittering in the night
The tree, glowing in the night with silver
Winter tree, bare in the day
Branches that have snow on
Frost that is beautiful
Trees dancing
Trees have ice on
Trees that have silver icicles.

Tyler English (6)
Long Sutton Primary School

MILLENNIUM

In the future I want to be
A person with lots of friends, 1, 2, 3
They might be smart
They might be dumb
They might not have a finger or a thumb.

I want to go in a spaceship to Mars
I want to invent lots of flying cars
They fly around space
And straight past your face.

I wish everyone understood
There are people on the streets
Covered in mud.
There are doctors that care
And are always there
And people with cuts on their knees
The doctors will get rid of the disease.

Joshua Seale (10)
Long Sutton Primary School

WINTER TREE

When I went to the woods
I saw this sparkling tree.
The leaves had fallen off the tree
It was a bare tree.
The snow, sparkling in the sun.
The grass was silver and wet.
On the way back the sun came up
and melted the snow.

Dale Wells (6)
Long Sutton Primary School

SNOWMAN

S nowflakes are falling down on the garden.
N ow we get on the sledge out from behind the shed.
O nce it's out, we slide along the snow on the grass.
W hoops! I fell off the sledge. I'm covered in snow.
M ist is here, I can't see. It is freezing in the mist.
A snowball hits me. My naughty brother threw it at me.
N ice watery hail falls on my head.

Joe Neaverson (7)
Long Sutton Primary School

SNOWY WINTER DAYS

When it's snowing, it is fun
I can throw massive white
fluffy snowballs
and I play with my brother outside
and throw snowballs at my
brother and my mum has to
clean him up.

Thomas Holmes (6)
Long Sutton Primary School

ICICLES

I cicles hanging,
C old and freezing,
I ce has come,
C old, crunching and damp,
L onging for summer to come,
E ven the ice is melting,
S now is melting.

Samuel Riggs (7)
Long Sutton Primary School

COLOURS

What is yellow?
The sun is yellow blazing at the crumbly soil.
What is blue?
The rivers are blue, softly flowing by.
What is green? The grass is green swaying in the wind.
What is white? A seagull is white swooping through the sky.
What is red? A rose is red standing straight and tall.
What is orange? The sand is orange on an exotic beach.
What is silver? The sea is silver in the sunlit evening.
What is purple? A bunch of grapes is purple on Spanish vines.
What is gold? My earrings are gold, glittering in the light.

Now you know how colourful the world is.

Elizabeth Grant (8)
Long Sutton Primary School

SNOWFLAKES

S   nowflakes come from the sky.
N   o one goes outside, it is freezing.
O   n the snow there are footprints.
W   aiting for my warm dinner.
F   ootprints are scary.
L   ying in the snow is freezing.
A   ll girls and boys come outside.
K   icking the snow.
E   ating hot dogs on cold days.
S   nowmen all around me.

Molly Day (7)
Long Sutton Primary School

TONGUE

Slippery wet
slimy soggy
tongue. Pink
tongue popping
in and out, up
and down,
round and
round your lips
licking viciously
at its favourite
food, slurping
its drink.

Harriet Smith & Stephanie Powell (7)
Long Sutton Primary School

BONFIRE NIGHT

The fire flames going into the dark night
sky and disappearing.
Then a firework is lit with a match and it
zooms into the sky.
Bang! All the beautiful colours
light the sky and it falls to the ground.
All the fireworks have gone
but we've still got the fire.
And now the people are coming to see
the bonfire.

James Bass (7)
Long Sutton Primary School

WINTER

W hile the snow starts to go
I   ce goes on the ponds.
N ow the trees start to glow.
T   he icicles float down like flies.
E   very snowflake falls down.
R   obins roost day and night.

Joshua Wilkinson (7)
Long Sutton Primary School

WINTER

W hite trees get blown by the wind.
I   cy trees shivering in the night.
N ow the winter birds start to fly.
T   he icicles start to sparkle.
E   very day the glittering snow starts to fall.
R   obin redbreast flies in the snowy skies.

Sophie Wise (7)
Long Sutton Primary School

WINTER TREE

Winter tree is so frosty and silver
When the wind blows and dances
The tree begins to get cold
The animals start to hide
The tree twists about
All the leaves are on the ground
Covered in snow and frost.

Katie Ingham (6)
Long Sutton Primary School

A WINTER TREE

Waving and blowing tree
It sparkles with frost
It looks like it is dancing
It is bare
Its twigs wave like arms
It is cold
It waves, some leaves fall
Leaves falling down
Sparkling so bright in the sky at night
It is covered in snow
When the wind stops it is still.

Chloe Ingham (6)
Long Sutton Primary School

WINTER

W   inter is cold
I   cicles hang
N   ight frosts
T   rees, bare
E   verywhere is covered with snow
R   obins stay but swallows go.

Marcus Miller (6)
Long Sutton Primary School

WINTER SNOW

Coating layers of snow are showered down to the soil.
Snow plunges down to the bitter cold, dark earth.
Snowflakes tumble down from the sky onto the ground.
The piercing winter is here.

Victoria Rayment (10)
Long Sutton Primary School

WINTER TREES

I can see the trees
Sparkling in the sunshine.
They are beautiful
With silver ice on their branches
I see trees waving about.
Trees looking frosty.
The leaves are falling down
On a winter day.

Amelia Winch (6)
Long Sutton Primary School

WINTER

W inter is pretty and fun.
I   like to play in the snow.
N ew beautiful frost
     patterns on the window.
T he snow is freezing and cold.
E veryone slides on the ice.
R unning in the cold snow.

Melanie Watts (6)
Long Sutton Primary School

DUNKIRK BEACHES

I think of dying friends lying on the beach,
I wait for the boats while I stand in the freezing cold sea,
I take off my overcoat weighing me down.
The boats have finally arrived, I jump on,
Still I think of my friends on the sandy beach.

Lianne Brimicombe (9)
Long Sutton Primary School

WINTER

W inter is so much fun and
children make patterns with their feet
I cicles hang from a house.
N o one is going outside tonight
T he snow is cold and the
snow is white.
E veryone is freezing cold
R acing snowflakes are falling down.

Rachel O'Sullivan (6)
Long Sutton Primary School

WINTER

W inter is good because we can throw snowballs.
I n winter it is freezing.
N one of the people are going outside.
T he snow falls from the sky.
E ven now people are riding their sledges.
R abbits are shivering with coldness.

Nicholas Godleman (6)
Long Sutton Primary School

WAR POEM

Here I am sitting on the freezing cold beach
Feeling alone even though there are
Thousands of people all around me,
I'm looking out towards the fierce sea,
I'm praying and hoping for a boat to come.

Jessica Burrell (10)
Long Sutton Primary School

WINTER POEM

Jewels hanging on the naked trees
They are cold and shivering like a person
They are twinkling in the cold, wet and dark air
Shining icicles hanging

The trees are swirling in the cold and wet air
The ice is dancing like a person
The trees are covering their friends
To keep them nice and warm

The silver and shining icicles disappear
But wind blows and blows and it never ends

The ice leaves slushy wet, cold and slushy
And Jack Frost calls out 'Goodbye.'

Gemma Wellard (10)
Long Sutton Primary School

SILVERY TREE

Trees shivering with coldness
Then they start to sway
Trees standing still and glittering
Doing the same every day
Trees dancing and singing
Twigs and stumps sparkling,
Branches and logs covered in frost
Icicles dangling from the tree
The trees look beautiful
On a cold frosty day.

Rebecca Navarrete (6)
Long Sutton Primary School

WINTERTIME

Frosty mornings, crisp and sharp.
Children skipping off to school.
Snowflakes falling from the sky.
Wintertime is back again.

Animals snoozing in their homes.
Trees, dead and bare.
Children dressed up warm and snug.
Wintertime is back again.

Robin Redbreast hops happily,
Everywhere white, frosty and bright.
Snowmen stand and never move.
Wintertime is back again.

Charlotte Blythe (6)
Long Sutton Primary School

WINTER

Winter is like a rabbit hopping around,
Here and there it works its magic,
Killing all the trees, or so it seems.

As it hops it creates an ice-cold path following it,
I observe the pathway that it has made,
We turn back and find an unfrozen tree
Which winter has yet to freeze.

It moves very slowly, like the winter's wind,
Every tree is frozen.
Still.

Elly Jackson (10)
Long Sutton Primary School

DUNKIRK POEM

Upon the cold, damp beach
At dreary Dunkirk
My best friend has just left this life.

Upon the dirty ship
We sail home
Sitting with no room to move our limbs
Everyone is tired.

Upon the joyous journey
Crashing through the water
We are all cheerful
For we can see our beloved homeland.

Thomas McEwan (10)
Long Sutton Primary School

KENNINGS POEM

A sky shiner.
A sunburn stinger.
An icicle melter.
A plant grower.
A body warmer.
A window steamer.
An ice-cream melter.
A green-grass grower.
    What is it?

Abbi Walker (9)
Long Sutton Primary School

ANCIENT EGYPT COLOUR

What is blue? The River Nile is blue
with crocodiles and hippos looking for their prey.

What is red? The Egyptian sun is red
burning people's skin.

What is white? The creamy white bandages
on mummies bodies are white.

What is yellow? The tall, sandy pyramids
covering the tombs are yellow.

What is black? The mushy and slushy
silt in Egypt is black.

What is green? A crocodile looking
for his colourful dinner is green.

What is grey? The feather of truth
balancing a gooey heart is grey.

What is purple? A flower being squeezed
to make a delicious perfume is purple.

What is gold? The Pharaoh's glittering,
shining crown is gold.

What is creamy? The thin, plain linen
that Egyptians wear is creamy.

What is brown? The Egyptians' dark
coloured skin is brown.

What is colourful? Why, the whole
of Egypt is colourful!

Amy Sheanon (9)
Long Sutton Primary School

DUNKIRK SEA

I have soldiers standing inside me with water up to their armpits.
I hear bombs whooshing down and I hear them hit the ground
And they make a terrible *bang!*
I look across the land.
I see injured or even dead soldiers
Just lying there
Left behind
Boats chug closer and closer
Will they ever make it in time?

Jamie Taylor (10)
Long Sutton Primary School

WINTER

The white, silver snow,
Is landing on the ground,
Pushing off all the crumbling leaves.
Massive icicles drop with sharp pointed ends,
I watch the glittering, silver snow falling from the sky,
The frozen ponds are covered with dying plants,
The trees stand there with all their leaves
Scattered all around.

Carrie Betts (9)
Long Sutton Primary School

MILLENNIUM POEM

I would like a healthy life,
I would like my sister to stop fighting me,
I would like more rock 'n' roll
I would like friends and to be happy

I would like for everyone to stop fighting
I would like no pollution
I would like new inventions
I would like schools to have more help.

Kay Blackbourne (11)
Long Sutton Primary School

WINTER

I am Winter,
I swoop around like a bird,
I freeze each web,
I see people making snowmen,
Then I create ponds, icy and stiff,
I like making people's toes numb, as numb as can be,
Trees are bare, they are shivering with cold,
Leaves are crumpled up,
They are lying on the floor.

Laura Ingham (9)
Long Sutton Primary School

AN AUTUMN EVENING

On a bitter, freezing night in autumn
The silver stars, shining brightly
The wolves, howling loud
Snow coming down like balls of thread
Ice hanging from the window
Crushing snow on the white ground
My fire keeping me nice and warm
In my house on an autumn night.

Thomas Pattern (10)
Long Sutton Primary School

KENNING

A small-creature
A creepy-creature
A climbing-winner
A bath-crawler
A sink-crawler
A ceiling-walker
A wall-climber
A fast-runner
A slow-runner
A hairy animal
       What is it?

Ben Beresford (10)
Long Sutton Primary School

A HARVEST POEM

Harvest is nearly here,
The wheat is rising,
It is flourishing in the golden sunshine,
The celebrations are about to start,
They are gathering food for the harvest table,
Stacked up like a mountain,
We see corn and barley growing,
Reaching up almost to the sky,
A sea of yellow waving hands,
Against the blue sky of morning.

Craig Tolliday (9)
Long Sutton Primary School

LEAVES

Autumn has come to stay forever
There is nothing worse than autumn's arrival
The sun no longer smiles down on the ground
Autumn has taken over.

There are many coloured leaves
Scarlet and golden
The odd shapes blowing around the sky
The leaves are sweeping, swooping high and low from the trees.

The trees shiver as the wind blows
Taking the leaves twisting and turning to the ground.

Tilly Bawden (11)
Long Sutton Primary School

WINTER

In the morning wind
It blew things around
It swept around me

In the snowy morn
It covered all the rooftops
It was so freezing

In the morning sun
It was burning all around
It grows every crop.

Toni Willows (10)
Long Sutton Primary School

A Kenning Poem

A memory builder
a game saver
a work producer
a letter writer
a people teacher
a paper printer
an e-mail sender
a picture maker
a shop on-liner
an electricity taker

What is it?

Michael Sealcoon (10)
Long Sutton Primary School

What Is It?

A water drinker
A wall creeper
An insect attractor
A slug feeder
A leaf builder
A trellis climber
A seed dispenser
A bud maker
A soil grower
A petal faller

What is it?

Jemma Wells (10)
Long Sutton Primary School

THE FROSTY SNOW

The ice is on the ground, it is glistening in the golden sun,
The trees are naked and wind sweeps the sky,
The icicles are hanging from the trees like a
glimmering crystal,
It's bleak and bitter outside.

Amy Walton (10)
Long Sutton Primary School

WINTER CINQUAIN

Winter
frosty morning
fallen snow on the grass
casting a sinister magic
everywhere.

Robin Anthony (10)
Long Sutton Primary School

WINTER

Icicles hang
Like the playing monkeys
Snowflakes drift swaying down to earth
Winter.

Lucy Busley 10)
Long Sutton Primary School

AUTUMN

The wind bites your toes in the autumn
The wind's bitter cold tongues lick your face
The wind rustles around the trees like mad
The leaves fall down from the trees like running water
The leaves change colour as the day goes on.

There are some rainy days about as well
Then the wind dawns on me.
Inside the house the fire gleams like a crystal
With its red and yellow colours about the room
I snuggle up next to it to keep warm
The whole house is warmer than a summer's day.

Luke Burton (10)
Long Sutton Primary School

MISTER SUN

An ice-dissolver,
                 a skin-smoulderer,
a sweat-maker,
                 a sky-brightener,
a seaside-crammer,
                 an ice-cream-dribbler,
a beach-swarmer,
                 a lolly-melter,
a child-fainter,
                 a sea-warmer,
        What am I?

Gary Simons (11)
Long Sutton Primary School

I HOPE . . .

I hope to live in a world
Where people look after the environment,
Where people walk to school instead of using cars,
Where people put their rubbish in the bin,
Where everyone cleans up after themselves,
Where farmers don't spray crops,
Where factories stop polluting the
Atmosphere with poisonous fumes
I hope to live in this world.

Hannah Rose (10)
Long Sutton Primary School

WINTER

His bitter blue hair bursts the sun.
The weather is Arctic.
He rushes past the icy cold cobwebs
Leaving a trail of frozen deadness
The snow melts as it hits the hard ground
Leaving a puddle of stone-hard frost.

Matthew Richardson (11)
Long Sutton Primary School

I HOPE . . .

I hope to live in a world where people
stop arguments about religion.
Where there is an end to wars and violence.
Where all people could live in harmony.
I hope to live in a world like this.

Ben Gardener (10)
Long Sutton Primary School

WINTER WEATHER

Snowdrops fall from the dark, gloomy sky,
They trickle down my face like teardrops,
Frozen icicles hang from the window ledge,
The ground is freezing cold.

Drizzles of rain drop from the dark sky,
The wind howls around my shivery body,
The ice crackles under my freezing feet,
Then the trees get blown around in the blistering wind.

Emily Barber (11)
Long Sutton Primary School

I HOPE . . .

I hope to live in a world
where people do not drop litter
making piles of rubbish in the street.
Where no oil is dumped in the sea
as the fish cannot swim.
People do not burn things,
filling the air with smoke.

Ashley Foulsham (11)
Long Sutton Primary School

I HOPE . . .

I hope to live in a world where
countries stop fighting with other countries
where there is no greed and violence so
people can roam free.

I hope to live in a world where
religion brings peace and joy
to the world and fighting ends.
I hope to live in this world.

Gemma Harrison (10)
Long Sutton Primary School

WINTER

The colours change from golden yellow to murky black
From everglade green to ice-cold white.
Bare trees shiver in the freezing wind,
Only evergreens stand with their warm coats
Of true green leaves.
No life is left in the grounds of the wood,
Plants try to shoot through the frozen, solid earth,
But they sink,
Like cowards,
Back to the warmth of their seed.

Nathan Guest (10)
Long Sutton Primary School

I HOPE...

I hope to live in a world
Where black and white
Can live and share the same world.
Where people are not judged
By their race or the colour of their skin.
Where different races can feel safe
To walk the same streets together.
This is the world I hope to live in.

Laura Fung (11)
Long Sutton Primary School

MILLENNIUM

In the future everyone will be,
A happy and caring person just like me,
They will live a healthy life,
Just like somebody's wife.

In the future I will be,
A healthy girl you will see,
I will be happy and have friends,
And lots of letters they will send.

In the future you will be,
A kind and gentle person just like me,
You will have lots of peace with no wars,
And they might even change the laws.

Victoria Penta Cawthorn (10)
Long Sutton Primary School

HAIKU

In the morning frost
It is slippery and cold
We go out to play

In the morning sun
We go outside to have fun
It sparkles all day

In the heavy rain
It fills up all the rivers
I don't like the storm.

Jade Wells (10)
Long Sutton Primary School

A MAGICAL CREATURE

Slowly floating through the still air,
A gentle fairy-like creature that calms the sky,
Magically changing the radiant colours to dullness,
Sad is she
As her snow tears run.
Falling delicately as she covers the world in a velvet blanket.
Trailing snowflakes and glimmering icicles,
That melt in the warm spring sky.

Danielle Sheanon (11)
Long Sutton Primary School

I HOPE

I hope to live in a world of peace and joy,
Where people aren't judged by the colour of their skin,
Countries can work together hand in hand without fear of war.
I hope to live in a world like this.

I hope to live in a world where everyone is equal
And has a right to stand up for what they believe in.

Amy Kettlewell (11)
Long Sutton Primary School

SPRING

In spring,
Flowers open
Their petals to the sun
Covering fields in the colours
Of hope.

Bethan Hasnip (11)
Long Sutton Primary School

I HOPE . . .

I hope to live in a world
Where everyone is equal,
No one should be rich,
No one should be poor.
Everyone should have a home,
No one should be homeless.
No one should be put in prison
For what they believe in.
Everyone should have food,
No one should starve.
No one should be called names
Just because they have a different coloured skin.

I hope to live in a world
A world of peace,
Where there are no wars
Fought in the name of religion.
Where we all live side by side
And get on with each other.
Where everyone can be friends -
A world of peace.

I hope to live in this world -
A better world!

Laura Hudson (10)
Long Sutton Primary School

WINTER GIRL

In the frosty morning,
When all is quiet and still,
Winter appears from out of nowhere
In her blue dress,
White diamonds in her hair.

In the icy afternoon,
When winter has kissed all the plants,
She turns around to see them die
From the poison on her lips.

Laura Coates (10)
Long Sutton Primary School

THE WIND

The wind, a great kingfisher
Darting round the countryside
He swoops high and low
Forcing leaves to descend down to the damp earth
Swirling, twirling, rotating
Gliding and skating in mid-air
Crimson, golden, amber coloured leaves
Slide slowly through the gentle breeze
A soft tune is heard as they fall
The melody of nature dying.

Ben Thompson (10)
Long Sutton Primary School

RAIN

The crashing of raindrops splattering on the window,
People outside put up their umbrellas,
As sudden downpours plunge on the world below,
The rain rampages like a furious bull,
People rush indoors to escape the mayhem,
Soon pools of water appear,
As the rain slowly ceases,
A rainbow appears.

Jack Hubbert (11)
Long Sutton Primary School

LIMERICK

There was an old man from Japan,
Who couldn't stop waving his fan,
He made such a draught
And no one else laughed,
They just hit him quite hard with a pan.

Jamie Tear (11)
Long Sutton Primary School

WINTER'S WEDDING

White confetti of snow
falls from the sky.
The misty sun in the bleak sky -
like a wedding ring -
a sign of hope.

Felicity Maynard (10)
Long Sutton Primary School

TEACHER, TEACHER

Teacher, teacher on a bridge,
Teacher, teacher on a sledge,
Teacher feeling very sick,
Got the hiccups, hick, hick, hick.

Teacher, teacher I am going to be sick,
Teacher, teacher come here quick.

Cheryl Newton (8)
St Andrew's CE Primary School, Leasingham

MESSAGE IN A BOTTLE

I was on holiday in New Zealand,
I went to visit my two best friends.
The sun was shining brightly,
As if it would never stop again.
We all went together for a midday stroll,
We decided to go to the beach.
We took along a picnic,
I had a juicy peach.
Just then in the distance,
I saw a shining thing.
It was a green glass bottle,
And it had something in.
We took out the letter,
And scribbled down a note.
Put it in the bottle,
And sent it off afloat.
We watched it duck and bobbing,
As it sailed off to the sea.
Until it hit a pirate ship,
That was sailing at full steam.
The pirates pulled it up on the deck,
And read aloud the note.
The note read that all pirates,
Were nasty little men.
And if they wanted a big fight,
They should come and see me then.
Just then my clock was ringing,
And I woke up in my room.
It was a very big shock to find,
That it had all been in my mind.

Jemma Trollope (11)
St Andrew's CE Primary School, Leasingham

ELEGY ON THE DEATH OF A PENCIL

When I was just a huge big tree,
Growing big and strong,
There was a girl at the age of three,
Who sang a lovely song.

But one day a man came along,
And sawed around my bough,
The man shouted, 'He's coming down,
Clear the way right now.'

Down I fell upon the ground,
Life was nearly over,
Off I went on a truck to my new home I thought,
Somewhere loud and noisy.

They stripped me down to something small,
And dipped me in some ink,
They boxed me up and put me on a truck again and again.

I sat upon a shelf at the local Woolworth's store,
Then a boy came along and took me from the back.
He said, 'It's the wrong one,' then he dropped me on the floor,
Memories of long ago, forests green and the little girl's song,
Have gone, have gone, have gone.

Amy Garwood (10)
St Andrew's CE Primary School, Leasingham

WHO DO YOU THINK YOU ARE KIDDING MR REDFERN?

Who do you think you are kidding Mr Redfern,
Even with a ding, dang, dong,
He will come with his big cane,
Oh, who do you think you are kidding Mr Redfern,
Even with a ding, dang, dong!

Who do you think you are kidding Mr Redfern,
Especially with a ding, dang, dong,
He will dress up in a soldier's suit,
And he will just lose one little boot,
Oh, who do you think you are kidding Mr Redfern,
Especially with a ding, dang, dong!

Simon Ross (9)
St Andrew's CE Primary School, Leasingham

THE DEATH OF A CRAZY TEACHER!

New teacher, is she strict, is she funny?
She came in the door holding a bunny,
The headmaster came and left her with us,
She said to us, 'My bunny is called Fuzz.'

She sat down slowly at her new desk,
Lizzy said 'Miss, it's time for our test.'
She turned music on and went berserk,
Dancing while we secretly smirked.

She started speaking to herself,
She's crazy, keep it to yourself,
The children were all very shocked,
Seeing her rocking in her socks.

Then she dropped down in her chair,
And started to say a prayer,
I said, 'I think she's dying,'
All the class started crying.

Then the headmaster came,
And said 'It's all a shame,
When you get a new teacher,
She's buried by the preacher.'

Alannah Clelland (9)
St Andrew's CE Primary School, Leasingham

ON A MONDAY AFTERNOON

It was a sunny Monday afternoon,
The kids were going wild.
There was Bertie, Alex, Luke and John
And Alex was getting tired.

John was the opposite to Alex,
Luke was just the same.
Bertie was watching the Ceefax,
The teacher was being a pain.

She whacked the children with a cane,
They thought they were going to die,
Later in the day,
It was the teacher who expired.

The kids were very sorry,
The kids were very sad,
The teacher had always told them
That one day they'd drive her mad.

The next day they all wondered
Who would take the teaching post,
When standing by the blackboard
To their horror, was a *ghost!*

Elizabeth Crawford (9)
St Andrew's CE Primary School, Leasingham

MY CAT MITTENS

My cat Mittens likes playing with his mouse,
He chases it and chases it all around the house,
He likes sleeping on my mum's settee,
And last night he stole some spaghetti.

My cat Mittens likes his food so much,
His favourite treat is probably Dutch,
After his food he likes a long nap,
In my uncle's very old comfortable cap.

Susannah McGagh (8)
St Andrew's CE Primary School, Leasingham

THE DEATH OF OUR TEACHER

The teacher was writing some sums on the board,
For all of us to do,
Trust me you don't want to do them,
There were one hundred and twenty two.

The chalk fell on the floor,
And the teacher tripped up,
She stumbled over,
And had a nasty cut.

The children all came running,
And jumped on her too,
The teacher was desperate,
She needed the loo.

She went to the toilet,
And banged her head on the door,
She fell onto the table,
And then onto the floor.

The teachers came outside
And saw her lying down,
Then I saw one of them
With a great big frown.

Liam Atkins (9)
St Andrew's CE Primary School, Leasingham

A POOR OLD GARDENER

A poor old gardener said 'Help me,
  My days are almost gone,
I've got arthritis in my knee,
  And now it's hard to run.

I've got a blister on my foot,
  And frostbite in my nose,
And help me if I haven't got,
  Pneumonia in my toes!

All my hair has fallen out,
  My teeth are in the bin,
I'm really getting rather stout,
  Although I'm much too thin!

My nose is deaf, my ears are dumb,
  My tongue is tied in knots,
And now my barrow and my spade,
  Have all come out in spots!'

Rebecca Ramsden (10)
St Andrew's CE Primary School, Leasingham

TROUBLE AFTER SCHOOL

At half-past three
It's goodbye to school
At last I'm free
I head for the pool

I have a good swim
But trouble comes in a bound
The lights have all gone dim
Oh help! There's no one around!

I struggled to the steps
And pulled my heavy weight out
I'm feeling all perplexed
'Is anybody there?' I shout

Praying I haven't been forsaken
Standing dripping like a drizzly day
For a fool I have been taken
Then a chorus of cheers - 'Happy birthday!'

Lisa Anderson (9)
St Andrew's CE Primary School, Leasingham

FOOTBALL CRAZY

Football is my favourite sport,
I am happy to report.

It's the greatest game of all,
Kicking a black and white ball.

When we go out onto the pitch,
There are a lot of shots we must not miss.

It takes a lot of foot control,
To score a brill goal.

Man U, Liverpool and Arsenal,
Look rather posh.

But when my team go out,
We make them look bad.

When we win we celebrate,
Then we go to McDonald's and stay out late.

Clare Hedley-Smith (11)
St Andrew's CE Primary School, Leasingham

SPOTS

Spots here, spots there
Spots - they are everywhere

Spots on your face
Spots on your bum

Spots are definitely
No fun!

Spots are big
Spots are small

Sometimes as big
As a *ball!*

All your pals
Laugh off their socks

When you have got . . .
Spots!

Mark Dowse (10)
St Andrew's CE Primary School, Leasingham

KOALAS

Furry and soft,
The little bears rest,
Clinging on trees,
Looking their best.

Eating eucalyptus leaves,
All crunchy and dry,
With their sharp claws
And then they give a sigh.

Christina Gould (9)
St Andrew's CE Primary School, Leasingham

FIRST DAY BACK AT BORING SCHOOL!

First day back at boring school,
All the teachers are playing pool,
The teachers are so boring,
Everyone started snoring!

John was being a pain,
So he got four strokes with the cane,
He wiggled his bum,
Bit off his thumb, oh no, not again!

It was soon lunchtime,
So the teachers watched us eat,
But we had to be careful,
Because they had cheesy feet!

When the headmaster
Came right in,
Everybody popped him,
With a pin!

Lee Stobart (8)
St Andrew's CE Primary School, Leasingham

RAINBOW

The rainbow, the rainbow
Shining so bright
The rainbow, the rainbow
It gives lots of light.

The rainbow, the rainbow
Gone for the night
The rainbow, the rainbow
Is now out of sight.

Jessica Sargeant (9)
St Andrew's CE Primary School, Leasingham

I'VE GOT A PET ALIEN

I've got a pet alien,
He's small and long,
He likes to get up to mischief,
When everyone's gone.

I've got a pet alien,
He likes me a lot,
When we play hide and seek,
He always hides in a pot.

I've got a pet alien,
He's weird and has a beard,
He comes from planet Zog,
And likes playing with Pogs.

I've got a pet alien,
He lives in my cupboard,
When I am asleep,
He nips downstairs for a peep.

Adam Woodmansey (9)
St Andrew's CE Primary School, Leasingham

BACK TO SCHOOL

The summer holidays are over
The garden's full of clover
We are back to school today
We're all back to school.

It's back to literacy this morning
You watch me I'll be yawning
After break, it's numeracy hour
Suddenly I've lost all my power!

Matthew Roope (9)
St Andrew's CE Primary School, Leasingham

WELCOME BACK TO PUDDING LANE SCHOOL

First day back in Pudding Lane,
Everybody's bored again,
Paul's trying to stay awake,
While Julie's trying to bake a cake.

Teachers giving out new books,
While cool school kids care about looks,
The teacher's just as boring,
While all the kids are snoring.

Teachers going half insane,
With children getting the smack of the cane,
A reception child whines,
While the teacher reads the daily times.

Five minutes till playtime comes,
Teachers are still smacking bums,
When the headmaster comes in,
Children hide behind the bin.

Tom Richardson (9)
St Andrew's CE Primary School, Leasingham

THE DRAGON DISCO DIVAS

In the deep dark sea,
Where all the dragons live,
There's a disco,
And they're all grooving,
Plus really, really moving,
They're having a great time,
Whilst drinking tuna brine.

Nicholas Hyde (9)
St Andrew's CE Primary School, Leasingham

MY GARDEN

My garden has creepy, creepy spiders
They live under the shed
Making their webs
Along comes a fly,
Yum, yum, here comes lunch

My garden has creepy, creepy toadstools
They're hidden in the grass
Making more
Along comes a person,
Squish, squash, *squish!*

My garden has creepy, creepy bees
They live in a beehive
Gathering honey
Along comes a bee
Pinch, pinch *ouch!*

David Martin (8)
St Andrew's CE Primary School, Leasingham

PET SNAKES

There was an old man called Jake,
Who owned a pet poisonous snake.
It bit off his head and now he's dead
So that was the end of Jake.

There was a young snake called Drake
Who started a fight with a rake,
It cut off his tail,
Drake went very pale,
And that is the end of my short tale.

Gerry Flynn (8)
St Andrew's CE Primary School, Leasingham

TIGER IN THE NIGHT

Cute in the morning,
Fierce in the night,
Eating in the dawning,
He's such a huge fright.

His stripes were big and black as coal,
His eyes were brown, raging with light,
He devoured his mouth against the foal,
And he ate it in the night.

In the morning sunshine he cleans his paws,
He prances along the rockery side,
He catches butterflies along the lawn,
When he chases a mouse he purrs with pride.

Rachel Fisher (10)
St Andrew's CE Primary School, Leasingham

COMING CAT

Among the bushes and the rushes,
Lies the coming cat.
Its long tail, male or female,
Is the coming cat.
Its clean paws forsaken indoors,
The poor coming cat.
Chases the bird that never heard
Cunning coming cat.
Eat the mouse planning for the house,
Never! Coming cat.
That cat loves the mats, come in, coming cat.

Alexandra Watt (9)
St Andrew's CE Primary School, Leasingham

THE TEACHER'S BAD DAY

There once was a teacher called Miss Flossy
She screamed and shouted all day long,
She was terribly, terribly, horribly bossy
And when she smacked she was awfully strong

She made us work in total hush
From start to end of a working day,
This made your brain just turn to mush
When school was out we yelled 'Way-hay'

One day Miss Flossy had a very sore throat
So the Head said to her 'You must go home,'
We made so much noise, we thought we would float
So home she went with a huge big groan.

Charlotte Elkington (9)
St Andrew's CE Primary School, Leasingham

MAGMAR

Magmar is a fiery creature
His head is golden brown
The flame on his tail protects
Him from animals that prowl around.

The flames on his body send out
A fiery blast and if you go near him
You will be on the floor
Dead fast.

Magmar is dangerous,
Magmar is fast
So if you see him
Run away extremely fast.

Jonathon Dunham (9)
St Andrew's CE Primary School, Leasingham

CHARIZARD

Charizad has fire on his tail
He drinks a lot of ale
And he burns all the mail
He tries to set sail

He blows out fire
Ruby red to catch the world's desire
But when he's not breathing fire
He gets higher and higher

Charizad has sharp teeth
For grinding meat
But this Pokémon has
Smelly feet.

Ryan Callaghan-Jarvis (8)
St Andrew's CE Primary School, Leasingham

JIGGLYPUFF

A small, happy, pink balloon,
Covered in fluff,
But when she gets angry,
She shouts '*Puff!*'

Jigglypuff is cute,
Jigglypuff is fat and round,
She blows herself up,
And starts flying around.

When Jigglypuff sings
She sends her opponents to sleep,
But when she loses,
She starts to weep.

Matthew Turner (8)
St Andrew's CE Primary School, Leasingham

THE HEADTEACHER

Children are big and small,
But some of them are tall,
The children do their work in class,
And play about with glass,
And in the playground they run about,
And scream and shout.

Some children are good,
Some are bad,
And some drive the teachers
Nearly mad.

We go to school every day,
Where we meet our friends,
To work and play.

Laura Taylor (9)
St Andrew's CE Primary School, Leasingham

THE MAD RAPPER

He's a mad man.
Fab man.
Rad man.
I'm glad he lives on our street,
He tells a rap to all the people he meets
And makes all the little birds tweet.
He raps, raps, rap all day long.
He raps until he has a knot in his tongue!
He has spiked up hair
And his jeans are torn.

Elliot Brooke (9)
St Andrew's CE Primary School, Leasingham

THE SUNSET APPEARS

The sunset is there,
Like a golden pear,
It follows me to the park,
While all the dogs bark.

The sunset is there,
It roars like a bear,
It is the best pet,
Of the set.

They used to call it the pet of the west,
It's the best,
It wears a golden vest,
While shining at its nest.

Penny Cheung (9)
St Andrew's CE Primary School, Leasingham

THE PHANTOM WHEELIE BIN OF THE NORTH

It looks like an ordinary bin on wheels
With numbers painted on in shocking white,
But if anything happens to meet it,
They won't get off light!
For underneath that innocent dustcart exterior,
Lurks a destructive evil force,
Before you know it it's after you with a vengeance,
Coming at you faster than a horse!
So if your lawnmower's stuck to the path,
Or your bike's been reduced to the size of a tin,
Now you know just what to say to everyone:
'It was the *phantom wheelie bin!*'

Emily Brown (11)
St Andrew's CE Primary School, Leasingham

DEAR WINTER

Why don't you let the sun shine on the Earth?
I hate the sun,
I can't stand it,
I can't stand it.
Like I can't stand
Fred Elliot,
So I try to block
It out, like you
Would with your
Enemy.

Why do you pour water from the sky?
When I find
Out on rainovision
That the sun is
Beating down on people
And drying up all their
Water, I feel sorry
For them and send water.

Why do you send flashing lights?
I send forks
Of lightning from
The sky because
When I get power
Over the sun, I
Get so happy
And when I
Say happy, I
Mean happy.

That I send
Forks of lightning
From the sky
To remind people
Of their nightmare
Sun.

Steve Sharp (10)
St Andrew's CE Primary School, Woodhall Spa

A RECIPE FOR MY BROTHER

Sprinkle
Sparkly stars drop in
Out of a tin
From the pub, The Old Inn.

Threw in
100 pieces of moon rock
Carved out of a black
With a knock!

Splat in
10 bottles of firework noise
Bubbles away in the pot.

Slobber in
108 gallons of blood
Bubbles away in the dark pot.
Slurp it
Gulp
Swish it
Gulp it
Then
Spew it!

Pamela Rayward (8)
St Andrew's CE Primary School, Woodhall Spa

FEELING

Why is the house so bare?
Where has my grandad gone, up there?
Why can't I hug him tight
And give him presents
And see delight on his face?

My nan is coming round today
Her tearful eyes
Look my way
She hugs me tight
I can't understand
She's like a rain cloud
But raining tears.

When the wind blows
I know he's there
He's telling me where to go
What to say and who to know
This Christmas my nan will be alone
For my grandad's dead.
There'll be one Christmas present this year.

Rebecca Lingard (10)
St Andrew's CE Primary School, Woodhall Spa

TANKS

The tanks engine burning, rushing to get to war
To earn his medal for his bravery.
People will tell other people about the tanks that won
The war and saved England.

The enemy waiting for the bang to end the war and their lives.

Guy Coupland (10)
St Andrew's CE Primary School, Woodhall Spa

EXTINCTION

White rhino stomps in the African waterfall.
Posh, shallow ladies chatting, 'Shall I buy these rhino beads?
Or shall I buy elephant beads?' She laughs. Not funny.
  The tiger wears his striped, fluffy coat

               one
                   last
                     time.

The whale swims in the Atlantic Ocean,
    not knowing any moment, he's lifted up
    and . . . very slowly
         put to death.
  All of them
       coats,
          horns
             and all.
  Shot by the terrifying,
             angry
     gun!
  Bang! Bang!
  and then . . .
  Extinction.

Grace Finney (11)
St Andrew's CE Primary School, Woodhall Spa

EYE

Wet watery tear dropping from my eye,
Splashing onto the cold floor.
My eye closed up and I wiped the wetness away.
My tear drop is shimmering silver,
It is a silver and blue emerald.

Harry Jackson (10)
St Andrew's CE Primary School, Woodhall Spa

THE LION STORM

Anger is a storm,
The storm is a lion,
That never stops roaring.

The lion has spotted its prey,
The chase is on,
The warthog must run.

Snap!
The lion has caught his prey,
The warthog is howling in pain,
Still trying to escape the clutches of the lion.

The warthog is dead,
No warthog.
The lion shivers away looking for
His next prey.

The storm is gone, all is calm,
Calm is happiness.

Chris Newstead (9)
St Andrew's CE Primary School, Woodhall Spa

FIRE

Fire is a burning dragon who roars non-stop
And flies over forests burning them down.
He eats wood, then hunts for more
He breathes on anything in his path,
He spits out little flames to make more,
His tail shoots around into the air
Cloaking the area in darkness.

Simon Da Silva (10)
St Andrew's CE Primary School, Woodhall Spa

DEAR STAR

Dear Star,
        Why does your sparkle
skip up the garden path?
Skipping is my best friend,
I play with it every darkness.
Why do you fade away when day
starts to dawn?
My night is your day and my
day is your night, I have to go
home to the higher heavens.
Why does your spark light up
the stretch of sky?
I have to do my fair share
of keeping the world satisfied.

If you're sad and low
just remember
my dazzle is your youth.

Alex Smith (10)
St Andrew's CE Primary School, Woodhall Spa

THE HAUNTED HOUSE

Creeping stairs and wooden doors, spooky howls from
Everywhere. Silky cobwebs, chipped paint, howling owls
In the trees, shattered windows, missing floorboards,
Smashed tiles,
Spooky vampires,
Dark, dark dungeon,
Scary skeletons, I'm scared!
Spooky, spooky, run, run, run!

Sam Dearie (9)
St Andrew's CE Primary School, Woodhall Spa

SADNESS IS . . .

Sadness is the howling sea who is depressed and
Feels his heart is empty and cold.
Happiness is a shooting star who makes giggly
Children gasp with perfectness.
Jealousy is the burning Devil, while everyone
Worships God.
Anger is the fiery sun, which tosses and turns
As no one dares to look at him.
Youth is a question which has no answer.
Light is an inspiring God who is fair as nature.
Dark is a sly, cocky witch who bubbles when
She is defeated.
Failure is a rare beast who lurches in the unknown forest,
Success is an unexpected bang which is
Heard from many miles away.
Cold is a shiver that makes its way up your bony spine.
Warm is a blanket which makes its way around you,
Till you're comfortable.

Belinda Pitwell (10)
St Andrew's CE Primary School, Woodhall Spa

A RECIPE FOR A FLAMING GHOST

Take six slimy snails
A slob of human blood
Four dead frogs
And add some flaming socks
With 8 burning people
And 12 stakes
Then taste it but don't waste it
And then pow! A flaming ghost appears.

Jamie Rickell (9)
St Andrew's CE Primary School, Woodhall Spa

BANG! BANG! BANG!

Swinging from tree to tree
Bang!
It was them, yes the poachers were back
The monkey knows it
Her heart beating faster than ever
She swings so fast
All she can hear in the background,
Bang!
Bang!
Bang!
Then silence . . .
The monkey's dead
Her baby cries as he's caught in a cage
All the baby can see in the distance is
His mum
Being taken away
To a land beyond the clouds.

Rachel Nelson (10)
St Andrew's CE Primary School, Woodhall Spa

SADNESS

That once playful image I once saw,
That sorrow with me, for sadness,
Once known,
That once image was my best friend,
I see that image in my mind, outside
Playing,
I wish it was there forever and ever
And come with me all the time, the
Place, the time.

Chris Wright (9)
St Andrew's CE Primary School, Woodhall Spa

DEAR SUN

Why do you shine on mostly our Earth?
My boy, that I cannot tell, it's to do with my birth.

Do you ever spin round any other planets?
No! I stick to the spot I was born in.

If a space shuttle comes near, do you
Turn up your heat to fry them?
No! I am not that cruel to Earth!
My default temp is 200°c!

Are you friendly with other stars and planets?
Why yes! Only I don't see them much, some I haven't even met!

Is it you who sends asteroids to Earth?
No! That is my rival: Starboy Birth!
Thank you for your time sun!
Bye!

James Ritson (11)
St Andrew's CE Primary School, Woodhall Spa

WHAT IS LIFE?

Sadness is a spooky ghost flying through Heaven.
Happiness is a party with balloons, cakes and friends coming to play.
Jealousy is a storm jealous of day.
Anger is a devil breathing fire in the depths of Hell, killing Hades.
Youth is a young boy running all day.
Light is a light bulb lighting up the dark cellar at night.
Dark is a forest waiting to trap lost tourists.
Failure is a boy who didn't pass his 11 plus.
Success is England winning the World Cup!

Chris Jelly (10)
St Andrew's CE Primary School, Woodhall Spa

DEATH

Why does death lurk in the mountains
Up in the highlands down by the shore
Why does death cause landslides, rockfalls
Why does death want to kill us all
Death is a disease, a germ, a scythe
Spreading destruction and losses everywhere
Treetops whisper, shivering and shuddering
Cold whispers of death are held in their lives
Death comes in a chariot of fire
Flames leaping and darting in his eyes
Death is like a black velvet clock
Covering things up hiding from glaring eyes
People yield to death's great powers
Falling down, down for eternity
The world is death's field, his oyster
His life.

Laura Cohu (9)
St Andrew's CE Primary School, Woodhall Spa

UP IN THE ATTIC

Damp, muddy woodwork,
Terrific dusty cobwebs,
Revolting blood and gore.
Greasy oil cans,
Vibrating rubber bands,
Giant dangerous nails.
Glass scattered all over the floor.
Punctured tyres,
Car engines
Mice scattering all over the floor.

Daniel Mehaffey (9)
St Andrew's CE Primary School, Woodhall Spa

SEA

The sea is a roaring lion
That roars at the sea bed
Scaring the fish away
Scratching at the rocky, rocky rocks
Like a hammer breaking a nail.

It sniffs at the shore and
Sleeps all day and night
The windows are rattling
The sandy shore crackling
That scares the children away.

But at night he quietens
You could hardly notice him
That is why he is
The prowling cat.

Daniel Gayton (10)
St Andrew's CE Primary School, Woodhall Spa

METAPHOR POEM

Swiftly swooping through the midnight sky
Breathing bright sparks of colour accompanying
The brittle shards of moonlight beaming down to Earth.
Carcasses of dead corpses falling
Without any life
Some with counter attacks in groups
Back in the capricious feeding ground
Baby siblings call for their mothers but
The only thing going to come is
Death!

Daniel Holland (11)
St Andrew's CE Primary School, Woodhall Spa

ANGER AND HAPPINESS

Anger is a lion fierce and large,
Chasing his prey,
He pounces onto the stripy zebra.
Tears the skin, rips the flesh,
Another lion comes,
A fight begins.
Lashing each other with
Razor-sharp claws.
One hobbles off like a paralysed man,
One is left.

Happiness is a female lion
Who has a baby,
Licking it joyfully,
Laughing at the clumsy baby
The wind playing a flute tune in the grass.

Tom Walsh (9)
St Andrew's CE Primary School, Woodhall Spa

LION CREEPING IN THE SNOW

A lion creeping in the snow,
Hunting for his prey suddenly
Everything went quiet.
Then he jumped
And snapped his teeth.
Crunching like a lion
Ripping a little baby rabbit
Blood dripping everywhere.
Then he walks away
Hoping he gets his next prey.

Lee Creasey (11)
St Andrew's CE Primary School, Woodhall Spa

DEATH

Who is she, playing at the stream?
I can't see her properly, only her shadow.
Where does she go as she gets to the end?

Somewhere I know
But where, I ask?

My eyes fill up like clouds of rain,
It's as if I was there again,
It seemed so strange and tickles my heart
The clouds go grey, I can't pull them back
I feel so hopeless and tearful.

Maybe I'll find her one day.

Just maybe.

Nicola Archer (10)
St Andrew's CE Primary School, Woodhall Spa

KENNINGS SCHOOL

Homework-giver
Ball-hitter
Lunch box-eater
English-poser
Maths-killer
Science-puzzler
Book-reader
History-maker
Art-heater
Board-wiper
Smelly-diaper
Don't worry, it's just our school.

Sherrissê Burnell (10)
St Andrew's CE Primary School, Woodhall Spa

SNOW IS . . .

Snow is a giant melting ice-cream,
Dripping to the tongue of the Earth
And splashing on the chocolate figures,
Leaving them in a soggy condition.

As the sun hits me I drip again
And again, again, again, again,
Soaking the chocolate figures more
And splashing their crispy covers.

Then cold comes I turn into creamy ice,
People love me and ice skate on me,
Cracking me, breaking me, smashing me
And turning me into water so I melt,
Away, away, away and away!

Claire Chapman (11)
St Andrew's CE Primary School, Woodhall Spa

FIRE

Fire is a dragon
That rumbles the ground
It spreads its wings
And makes fire all around.

The dragon glides through the air
And creatures dart out of the way everywhere
In the day he hides away
Waiting for everything to rot and decay.

Then once again when night is nigh
The king of the fire comes out to make creatures sigh.

Ben Hayden (11)
St Andrew's CE Primary School, Woodhall Spa

THE QUESTION OF LIFE

Polar bear how much do you care
Being locked up in a dinky cage?
I think it should definitely be banned
For I live in the sea
And should not be put in captivity.

Fox should you be hunted by me?
It should be banned straight away
I am so beautiful
So I should stay.

Whale how much do you care being made into shoe polish
And lipstick?
Of course I care, for I should not be put on painted faces
And should not be killed by you and me.

Joshua Keegan (9)
St Andrew's CE Primary School, Woodhall Spa

SADNESS

Raindrops slide down the branches
Trickling down to the ground
As do the tears falling beneath me.

Forces of wind blowing the leaves
Pushing them towards places of sorrow
Like losing the friction of happiness.

Dark clouds hollow around my world
Causing nothing but devastation.
As do my eyes closing and my mind
Setting the devil free to my life.

Arpege Neary (9)
St Andrew's CE Primary School, Woodhall Spa

DEATH

Why do I see a field stained with blood?
Why do I hear the sound of guns like thunder in my ears?
Why do I smell the smell of rotting flesh?
Why do I feel blood flooding from my wounds?
Why do I see barb wire fences?
Why do I hear blood chilling cries of pain?
Why do I smell the scent of gunpowder, floating
Through the air?
Why do I begin to feel weaker?

Why do I see black hands reaching out to grab me?
Why do I hear the call of death?
Why do I smell the scent of my grave?
Why do I feel a great weight upon my shoulders?

Daniel Malcolm (9)
St Andrew's CE Primary School, Woodhall Spa

DARK IS A . . .

Dark is a slick black horse
Galloping across the damp forest floor,
His rider whooshing past the unknown world.
The horse is running, running from the
Winter's sharp bite.
The world stood still, the racing winter
Has taken over.
A horse once known to run free, captured
By frosty hands of death, lies still as the
Winter cries a loud chilling laugh.

Ha! Ha! Ha!

Amy Loughe (9)
St Andrew's CE Primary School, Woodhall Spa

GRANNY

Through every nook and every cranny
The wind blew on a poor old Granny,
Around her knees, into each ear
(And up her nose as well as fear).

All through the night the wind grew worse,
It nearly made the vicar curse.
The top had fallen off the steeple
Just missing him and other people.

It blew on man, it blew on beast
It blew on nuns, it blew on priests,
It blew the wig off Auntie Fanny
But most of all, it blew on Granny.

Leon Leaney (9)
St Andrew's CE Primary School, Woodhall Spa

TEACHERS

Science   Puzzler
                   Word guzzler.

Board wiper   Wiper
                   Smelly diper.

Test marker   Getting darker.

Brain beater   Blood heater.

Work giver   Bone shiverer.

Head   Steamer.

Don't worry it's just a teacher!

Alex Smith (10)
St Andrew's CE Primary School, Woodhall Spa

TIGERS HAVE A RIGHT!

The beautiful tiger prowling through the forest,
He can run freely living happily in peace.
Bang!
There goes a gun
The clatter of horses hooves,
They gallop over the hills
Faster, faster, making the tiger tired
On and on making the tiger even more
Tired by the second.
Suddenly another gunshot goes, slowing
The tiger down!
Soon the horses are so close
The tiger can get trampled by them
Another gun goes
Slowly the tiger falls to the ground
The next day there is no tiger
Prowling the forest, no tiger running free
But a sad stuffed tiger dangling
From the ceiling.
A crowd watching
A few people get angry
Some children get upset
'How can we see this poor creature
Dead and stuffed?'
'Why do we do these awful things?'
They said,
'Our precious tiger dead,
Where shall we find another
Gift as precious as gold?'

Hannah Evison (10)
St Andrew's CE Primary School, Woodhall Spa

MY NEW YEAR RESOLUTIONS

I won't scoff all the food in the kitchen
Nor chop off my art teacher's head.
I will not send my dog to the moon,
Or put slugs in my bad brother's bed.
I'll never shout, spit, swear or scream
I'll do my best to be good,
I wouldn't paint my mum's walls with her make-up
Or splat my dad's car with mud.
I'd never fall out with my best friends
(Although I haven't got any)
My money will all go to charity
Every note, every pound, every penny. (Shame I'm broke)
I won't say no to doing the chores
I will eat up all my greens,
I'll try to resist the temptation
Of licking dessert plates clean.
I will not change the grade on my report card
Or throw the teacher through the door.
How dare you say I'd hit the class dork?
(But now I really want to even more!)
My resolutions, I will confide
In you to keep me going,
But I must confess, I'm in a mess
Without you knowing the truth:
I lied!

Sarah Browne (10)
St Andrew's CE Primary School, Woodhall Spa

THE DISASTER

Deers drinking the blue, clear water.
Tigers getting ready to pounce on the curious prey.
Birds chirping as they feed their young.
Fox cubs scamper and play here and there.
Elephants splashing in the muddy water, spraying each other
with their long, grey trunks.
Horses galloping as free as the wind, while rabbits sniff and play.
Then . . . *bang!*
Hunters come with trained dogs and guns, while horses
gallop as fast as their poor legs can carry them.
Tigers and rabbits run for the last time
while elephants and deers have their last look at the jungle.
A deer runs for his lost and lonely life, when *bang!*
Lots more guns shoot and shoot while the hunters leave
the animals to bleed to death.
Blood
    d
      r
       i
         p
          s
            to the floor from the dogs' teeth, where they bit the
animals' legs.
Will we ever find a crime like this?

Tammy Lai (11)
St Andrew's CE Primary School, Woodhall Spa

CLOUDS

Why oh why?

Why oh why
Do you get so angry?
I get so angry
Because you fly straight
Through me.

Why oh why
Do you make
Electricity bolts flash
So much?
I just like to
Make my own
Light so one day
I'll be stronger
Than the sun.

Why oh why
Do you threaten us
With hail?
I threaten you
With hail
Because you
Pollute me
So bad I
Get
Mad!

Ben Bradley (10)
St Andrew's CE Primary School, Woodhall Spa

YOUTH IS . . .

Youth is a beautiful flower,
That grows in the sun.
The flower needs a touch of life by water,
All the other flowers have long lives as adults,
But the flower of youth still grows,
The sun teaches the flower to grow
And helps it all the way,
The thoughts are beneath the plant,
But its greatest fear the frost has come
But it's survived this one.
The flower of youth is full of surprises,
That secret will never be let out.

Ellie Finney (9)
St Andrew's CE Primary School, Woodhall Spa

UP, UP AND AWAY

U   p in the sky is a dream,
P   roud and happy up there,

U   p in the sky must be magic,
P   assing the fluffy white clouds,

A   millennium would be a wonder up there,
N   ever do you have to be afraid,
D   own here, there isn't much to see,

A   nd up there, well, it's fascinating,
W   hether or not you go up there,
A   lways have a look up there,
Y   ou'll love the sky, I promise you.

Up, up and away!

Hannah Longhurst (9)
St Augustine's Catholic Primary School, Stamford

IF I COULD BE

If I could be a robin with a breast red, as red as could be,
I'd fly around the garden performing my show for all to see,
If I could be a butterfly with beautiful coloured wings,
I'd fly gracefully through the blue sky and I'm not telling a lie.
If I could be a giraffe with a wonderful long neck,
I'd be able to see the sky so I'd peer over the
Rooftops and watch the clouds go by.
If I could be a leopard with those charming
Chocolate spots I'd be able to catch a big
Gazelle and eat lots and lots.
If I could be a tiger with lots of handsome stripes
I'd prowl around the forest looking for time to strike.
If I could be a chimpanzee with pink knuckles for me
I'd swing silently through and look for a honeybee.

But really I like being me.

Harry Offer (9)
St Augustine's Catholic Primary School, Stamford

UP, UP AND AWAY

I want to go in a hot air balloon,
Now I have the chance
To go in with you,
What a lovely view
From the sky!
It was a lovely summer's day,
It was getting brighter on the way.
Then it was time to land
On the ground,
It was a time to remember!

Hannah Cowley (9)
St Augustine's Catholic Primary School, Stamford

STAR WARS

Wwwoooosh! As fast as lightning!
The battle droids are armed with blaster rifles
Battling and destroying Queen Amidala's city,
But here come the Naboo fighters,
Pow, pow, pow, down on their knees the droids go.
Here come the Jedi Knights
Called Obi-Wan and Qui Gon Jinn
Killing one hundred droids off their back with one light sabre.
Wwwoooosh! The Empire blows up the entire housing for
Tractor beam generator and secondary docking arms.
In fact everything blows up and all that's left is a noise,
That goes wwwoooosh and everything else is just dust except
Queen Amidala's planet.
So no more bad guys.

Alexander Holland (9)
St Augustine's Catholic Primary School, Stamford

FIREWORKS!

The fireworks go *Bang! Crackle! Crackle!*
Different types, Catherine wheels turn and look wonderful,
Rockets are very loud and go *Bang!*
You can see sparks in the sky
Some go *Bang!* Some are bright.
You can have lit-up dinosaurs, animals and whales.

Sparklers are small,
If you write your name in the sky
It turns out smoke.

Fireworks are fun but they are dangerous.

Robert Mohan (8)
St Augustine's Catholic Primary School, Stamford

NAUGHTY, NAUGHTY

There was a naughty girl
And she did something bad
She went into the staffroom
And the teachers went mad

She ran away from school
And went home
And she phoned to get tickets
To go to the Dome

The bill was a lot
And she got into trouble
But she didn't care
She just blew a bubble

She had learnt her lesson
And didn't get into trouble anymore
She got tempted and when she did
She fell on the floor!

Hollie Dalgleish (9)
St Augustine's Catholic Primary School, Stamford

A DREAM

One night when I was fast asleep,
Under my cosy warm sheet,
I was flying in the sky,
Saying goodbye to a beautiful butterfly.
I saw some people down below,
Dancing upon the shimmering snow,
Also I saw a sparkling stream,
But I stirred, it had all been a dream!

Olivia Cliff (7)
St Augustine's Catholic Primary School, Stamford

Up, Up And Away

'Up, up and away,'
Said Daddy on the day
Of rugby's greatest fixture.
In the car and on the way.

The ball became a missile
When the referee blew his whistle,
It soared toward the Heavens
At the Middlesex rugby sevens.

It went into an orbit
We hardly even saw it,
Until it came back down again
To feature heavily in the game.

Then home to tea and angel cakes,
Which only Mum's allowed to make,
Then chat about the day we've had,
A great big thanks to our kind dad.

Josh Goodwin (9)
St Augustine's Catholic Primary School, Stamford

Poppies

To and fro the poppies blow,
Their red heads, bowing low.
As the gentle wind pushes them from side to side,
I'm surprised that they don't seem to mind.
In their field, quiet and still,
Just watching them is quite a thrill.
To and fro the poppies blow,
Their red heads, bowing low.

Jenifer Wilson (9)
St Augustine's Catholic Primary School, Stamford

WELCOME TO CHOCOLATE LAND

Welcome to Chocolate Land, Chocolate Land,
Chocolate Land,
Where I'm drinking chocolate mousse.

There is chocolate down the loo,
There is chocolate in the poo,
All the animals in the zoo
Are all made of it too.

The servant is serving fish
On the very best dish,
On the muddy swamp
While they all chomp.

All the animals like to play
As they all like to say

Come back, come back, come back.

Sarah Clare (10)
St Augustine's Catholic Primary School, Stamford

WHAT THE STORM DID

It threw down the trees and it pulled up the grass.
It threw up a shipwreck without its mast.
It pulled down half the cliff.
What a terrible place it was, where the trees were on the floor,
The grass was all torn up, half the cliff was on half of the beach.
But what a brilliant sight it would be, to see the shipwreck.
That's what the storm did.

Catherine Scutts (8)
St Augustine's Catholic Primary School, Stamford

My Colourful World

The clouds are white
like cotton wool.
The grass is green
soft and clean.
The daisies are like
a carpet of flowers.
Dandelions are yellow
and bright.
The trees are high
they hide the sky.
The birds are sweet
all fluffy and cute
singing sweetly as
morning comes.
The sun so bright
it hurts your eyes.
The man on the moon
waves goodnight.
Tomorrow comes all over
again, the same thing
happens again and again.

Ruth Tucker (8)
St Augustine's Catholic Primary School, Stamford

Space

A big hole in the solar system,
As black as the night sky.
All the white balls of gas above our heads.
A yellow ball as hot as the middle of the Earth.
When the sun comes to rise the black night sky comes to die.

Alexander Tkaczyk-Harrison (8)
St Augustine's Catholic Primary School, Stamford

FUNFAIR OF THE MICRO-ORGANISMS

Spines on my back, I intend to go far,
Run into a road an' get squashed by a car.
When I curl into a ball, I go very slow,
But when a monster truck turns up,
I really start to go.
I'm not a dog, I'm not a log,
As you may of guessed I'm a flat hedgehog.

Tusks on my face, I may poke you up the bum,
I have no fingers and have no thumbs.
I have a ten metre trunk, and ears like plates,
And if I sit on you, you'll be flat like a pancake.
I'm fat and cute, but that's irrelevant,
As you may have guessed, I'm an elephant!

Richard O'Brien (9)
St Augustine's Catholic Primary School, Stamford

A TRIP TO THE SUN

Burning like a scolding rock,
Steam rising like a glooming fog,
Fire rising, burning hot,
Mist swirling, cool it's not.

Hard and strong, steaming hot,
People can't go, it's too hot,
Safe is it? No it's not!
Am I going, no I've forgot.

It's too hot!

Melissa Walton (8)
St Augustine's Catholic Primary School, Stamford

THE BIG KICK!

Up, up and away,
The rugby ball is kicked to Zimbabwe,
It hits a man on the head,
So he falls on the floor because he's fainted.

I wonder why he kicked the ball away to Zimbabwe,
For it hits a man,
So his head's like a frying pan.

The angry, agile, annoyed and alerted boy kicked the ball to . . .
Wait for it . . . Bombay.
I wonder if this time someone flies away,
By going up, up and . . . away!

Dominic Jones (9)
St Augustine's Catholic Primary School, Stamford

THE ELEPHANT

A long, swaying nose
and fat, chunky toes.
Big, floppy ears
and very slow gears.
A very short memory,
he'd forget his 'dilemary'.
Grey wrinkled skin
and tusks on his chin.
'Cause his tusks are made of ivory,
hunters are his rivalry.
I might not be intelligent,
I'm a special grey elephant.

Sam Peachman (10)
St Augustine's Catholic Primary School, Stamford

IDEAS FROM MY PAINT BOX

Black is when my eyes close,
Black is when a pen glides across the paper,
Black as night falls on the Earth.

White is a cloud floating by,
White is a candle burning in the night,
White as the snow falling down.

Blue is the bright sky during the day,
Blue is the colour of my chair,
Blue is part of the rainbow.

Yellow is for buttercups which are so nice,
Yellow is for the sun which blazes down,
Yellow is for custard that is so yummy.

Green is for trees which grow so big,
Green is for the lights, so go, go, go,
Grass is green, so how do you seem?

Gold is the colour of my dad's wedding ring,
Gold is the colour of my mum's earrings,
Gold is the colour of my goldfish.

Silver is the lining of the clouds,
Silver is the colour of the loose change in my pocket,
Silver is the colour of my bike keys.

Lucy Tucker (11)
St Augustine's Catholic Primary School, Stamford

UP, UP AND AWAY!

Up, up and away
The aeroplane goes,
Past birds, past clouds,
And then down, down it goes.

Phoebe Cliff (7)
St Augustine's Catholic Primary School, Stamford

I'M NOT SCARED
(I thought I wasn't scared of anything until one day . . .)

The wind was whirling
And the window was creaking
The curtain was flying
I thought I was dreaming
While I walked, the carpet was having a squeak
Still I dared myself to have a peek
The drawer slang out
The wind was still having a shout
I was hoping that another squeak
And I would have a peek
I put my hand on the window
To have a go
My fringe was no more a fringe
As the door came off the hinge
It was terrifying
And my mind was crying
How I possibly got out of bed
I couldn't say
Not even after having to finish chewing off a pencil lead
I really wish I could now lay
On my bed.

Md Inamul Ahmed (10)
Seathorne Primary School

THE FOUR TIGERS

The four tigers
Sitting in a tree;
One became a lady's coat -
And now there are three tigers.

Three little tigers
Beneath a sky of blue;
One became a poor man's rug -
Now there are two tigers.

Two little tigers
Sitting in the sun,
One's a hunter's trophy made -
Now there's only one tiger.

One little tiger
Waiting to be had,
Oops! He got the hunter first -
Aren't you kind of glad.

Vicky Copley (11)
Seathorne Primary School

HAPPINESS POEM

Happiness is hugging your mum,
Happiness is doing homework,
Happiness is a new pair of trainers,
Happiness is joining in a game with your friend,
Happiness is doing science,
Happiness is eating sweets,
Happiness is going to bed,
Happiness is playing football.

Dale Amies (9)
Seathorne Primary School

MY VALENTINE

Baby baby you're so fine,
Baby baby say you'll be mine.
Baby baby let's make this true,
Baby baby by saying *I love you.*
Baby baby let's dance by candlelight,
Baby baby you and me, what a marvellous sight.
Baby baby I think of you every night and day,
Baby baby help me chase these shadows away.
Baby baby how about a meal?
Baby baby how do you feel?
Baby baby what do you think?
Baby baby sit down please have a drink.
Baby baby I'll leave you never,
Baby baby our love is forever.

Connie Overton (11)
Seathorne Primary School

YELLOW BUTTER

Yellow butter, purple jelly
Red jam, black bread
Now repeat it while you eat it

Yellow butter, purple jelly
Red jam, black bread
Spread it thick, say it quick

Yellow butter, purple jelly
Red jam, black bread
Don't talk with your mouth full . . .

Harry Clare (10)
Seathorne Primary School

OFF TO THE SHOPS

We're off to the shops
And there's lots to buy,
We can buy:

Rich, red apples
Yummy, yellow bananas
Terrific, tasty chocolates
Handsome, harsh donuts
Fresh, fair eggs
Fantastic, fine fish
Great, green grapes
Helpful, handy ham
Icy, imaginative ice-creams
Jiggy, joyful jelly.

These will tickle your taste buds!

Joanna Kay Crooks (9)
Seathorne Primary School

FRIENDS

Friends, friends, they always care,
Friends, friends, they're always there,
Friends, friend, they're really kind,
Friends, friends, the ones I've got are hard to find,
Friends, friends, they make you laugh,
Friends, friends, they're really daft,
Friends, friends, they're really mad,
Friends, friends, don't make you feel sad,
Friends, friends, I'm just glad they're mine!

Laura Geaghan (11)
Seathorne Primary School

HAPPINESS

Happiness is school,
Happiness is a swimming pool,
Happiness is a sister,
Happiness is a brother.

Happiness is cooking,
Happiness is talking,
Happiness is books,
Happiness is jokes.

Happiness is new things for the rest of the day,
Happiness is going on holiday,
Happiness is . . .

Habibah Yasmin (8)
Seathorne Primary School

THINGS THAT HAPPEN IN THE SEA

The sea is flowing,
The boats are rowing,
The waves are curling,
The dolphins are twirling,
The seals are playing,
Their friends are spraying,
Their tails are waving,
The fish are slaving,
The jellyfish are wobbling,
Like a dog's tail flapping.

Amy Willard (11)
Seathorne Primary School

MY SHOPPING LIST

We're off to the shops
And there's lots to buy,
We can buy vegetables
And fruits and potatoes.
Jam and ham and
Lamb, turnips and all,
Everything you could think of.
Jam went with Sam, and cucumber,
Some beans are to be seen
With spaghetti and Betty,
Apples with sandals, Mars bars
And toy cars.
Pears and teddy bears and
clothes to wear.
Bananas and piranhas
And Tara's new trainers.

Jordan Cooper (8)
Seathorne Primary School

HAPPINESS

Happiness is getting a hug from my family,
Happiness is a great friend,
Happiness is going to America,
Happiness is winning a race,
Happiness is having a break from school,
Happiness is beating the score on the computer,
Happiness is playing football,
Happiness is having a take-away,
Happiness is listening to music.

Jessica Lindley (8)
Seathorne Primary School

WHATEVER THE WEATHER TODAY!

It's a horrible, dull, rainy day,
But wait until the season of sunny May,
When we can have lots of fun,
Playing all day long in the beautiful sun.

When winter comes and the snow is falling,
We have fun, but then tea's ready and Mum's calling,
On the beach the sun shines on the sea,
While I lay thinking of the beautiful weather with glee.

So whatever the weather, I don't mind, come sun, rain, snow or wind,
I'm happy all the time.

Adam Haywood (9)
Seathorne Primary School

HAPPINESS

Happiness is when you win a game of football,
Happiness is when you get some money,
Happiness is when you get some sweets,
Happiness is when you get some books for your folder,
Happiness is when you fill your book,
Happiness is when you are at school,
Happiness is when you are in goal,
Happiness is when you go to maths,
Happiness is when you finish your work,
Happiness is when you go swimming,
Happiness is when you are on the computer.

Jessegaron Verheul (9)
Seathorne Primary School

SLIP SLAP

S lip slap slop, down the rain drops.
L ip lop lap, down the rain taps.
I ppi oppi appi, the rain is slappi.
P lap plop plip, down I slip!
S lip slop slap, on my lap.
L ip lop lap, on my cap.
A p op ip, I take a sip.
P ip pap pop, the rain stops!

Jeordie Ringsell (10)
Seathorne Primary School

IN THE KITCHEN

In the kitchen
The pots go clang
And the dishes sang,
While glasses go tang,
Then the cooker goes bang,
The microwave rang,
For the lemon meringue,
Then we all sang.

Todd Bangham (10)
Seathorne Primary School

THE BLAZING DAFFODILS

From a little bulb in the ground that is dark like a
cave and as cold as an iceberg, the little tiny
shoot shot like a dart into the air.
Spring is here. The birds build a brilliant bright proud
nest. Then the buzzing bright bees buzz around.

Jason O'Hara (11)
Seathorne Primary School

OFF TO THE SHOPS

We're off to the shops and there's lots to buy.
We can buy
Large beds or doll's heads.
Banana skins and small pins.
Sweets and shiny shoes that fit on my feet.
Pretty hats and furry cats.
Lots of games with different names.
Garden tools and paddling pools.

Emma Bagnall (8)
Seathorne Primary School

WET PLAYTIME

There was a boy who wanted to play all the time when it was wet play,
But all he had to do was play with clay.
When the boy wanted to go outside, he couldn't
Because sploshing down, the rain came,
Like a pain.
One day the boy went out to play when it was sunny.
He was pulling a face like a bunny.

Vern Bee (8)
Seathorne Primary School

THE INVISIBLE MAN'S INVISIBLE DOG

The invisible man's invisible dog
Could look like a rabbit or even a hog,
It may look like a pig or maybe a cat
Or even a hamster but not a rat,
But no one knows for they're invisible,
Where do they live? Is their house invisible?

Sarah Smith (10)
Seathorne Primary School

OFF TO THE SHOPS

We're off to the shops
And there's lots to buy.
We can buy
Amazing apples, red, yellow and green,
Fine, pinky beetroot in a sealed jar,
Big, fat coconuts on sale in store,
Huge, fluffy dumplings ready for a stew,
Double-yolked eggs in a pack of six,
A big pack of raising flour, ready for the oven,
A green, big bunch of grapes going in our mouths,
Two, big pieces of holly ready for Christmas,
A pack of icing going on the wedding cake,
Three bottles of orange juice for the kids,
Something for their packed lunch, I know, KitKats,
Some flavourings for the food, lemons and limes,
Rich salad cream, mayonnaise, that's what we need,
I like noodles, fresh, fresh noodles,
Greasy olive oil, sprinkle, sprinkle, sprinkle,
One big, fat, plump pineapple,
Chocolate I need, for Mum, Quality Street,
I hate rhubarb but it is not for me,
Scampi likes scampi so I might as well buy it,
Trifle for my sister's party,
The cheapest ice-cream is Vienetta.

Cassie Dreher (9)
Seathorne Primary School

OFF TO THE SHOPS

We're off to the shops
And there's lots to buy.
We can buy
Some juicy apples,
A couple of dates,
A dozen eggs,
One fresh fig,
A juicy bunch of grapes,
A horrible hip, that I don't like,
A tub of vanilla ice-cream,
A bottle of juice with Tarzan on the front,
A couple of rough-skinned lemons,
Two blueberry muffins,
Three packets of curly noodles,
A bag of orange oranges,
Lots of ripe peaches,
Quinces that I don't like again,
Ten raspberries because we don't all like them,
A packet of strawberries which have little bits inside them,
Twelve tangerines for the party tonight,
Two fat, juicy watermelons,
And last of all my favourite, a yam.

Laura Hamilton (9)
Seathorne Primary School

HAPPINESS

Happiness is achieving something,
Happiness is winning a race,
Happiness is a friend,
Happiness is a chocolate doughnut,
Happiness is football,
Happiness is playing on your PlayStation,
Happiness is having a dog,
Happiness is a cuddle from Mum,
Happiness is a present from me to you,
Happiness is making a game,
Happiness is work that is never boring,
Happiness is a board game,
Happiness is your birthday,
Happiness is Christmas,
Happiness is a medal,
Happiness is karate,
Happiness is passing a test,
Happiness is sweets,
Happiness is a family,
Happiness is food,
Happiness is a brother or sister,
Happiness is fun we share,
Happiness is boyfriend or a girlfriend,
Happiness is at Easter,
Happiness is a story,
Happiness is a drink,
Happiness is the weather,
Happiness is laughing,
Happiness is when you sleep,
Happiness is a dream.

Glenn Browne (9)
Seathorne Primary School

WET PLAYTIME

Wet playtime means chatter, chatter!
Nitter, natter, want a game of chess?
Nothing else interests us more than a game of chess.

 Chatter, chatter,
 Nitter, natter,
 Chatter, chatter,
 Natter.

At the end of playtime we all go to maths,
Maths is hard, hard is maths.
That's the end of playtime.

 Chatter, chatter,
 Nitter, natter,
 Chatter, chatter,
 Natter.

Liam Topliss (8)
Seathorne Primary School

SHAPE POEM

  Spring returns,
  Shoots come up,
  Summer burns,
  Garden life,
  Autumn's turn,
  Trees sleep now.

Winter here,   But as we
No life near,   Know Christmas is next.

Elliot Smith (8)
Seathorne Primary School

THE ALLEY CAT

I may be an alley cat
But
Here is an interesting fact,
My relative is the *Lion King*
Is that not an amazing thing?

I may live on the wrong side of the track
But
Apart from Antarctic and the Outback
My wild cousins live in every corner
I often miaow to Scottish Aunt Lorna!

I may have to hunt for my dinner
But
With my claws and teeth, I'm always a winner!
I walk on velvet tippy toes
Bad for mice and other foes.

I may not have pedigree looks
But
According to all the very best books
I'm sleek and handsome, full of grace
So what if I have a battleground face!

I may not know who my grandparents were
But
I do have attractive marmalade fur
Thanks to them I'm cleaner and fast
Built like a tank, I'm going to last!

I may be a mangy old tom
But
It will take more than a nuclear bomb

My first was a very ancient cat
Now I'm millennium again!
How's that?

Robbie Mitchell (9
Staniland Primary School

SPOOKS

In my bed at night
In the dark without my
Light, I see ghosts and
Ghouls and vampires that
Bite. Skeletons rattle their
Bones, zombies walk the night
It's such a terrible, terrible sight.

Under the blankets, I
Hide, with my favourite
Teddy at my side. I hope
It's all a dream and
I'm fast asleep, no more
Goblins or ghosts for
Me to peep.

The sun was shining
Through my window I
Took a little peer,
The spooks are no
Longer here!

Rosa-Marie Woods (9)
Staniland Primary School

THE FRUITS OF LIFE

Apples keep the doctor away,
Bananas make you see each day,
Cherries make you smile with glee,
While dates make you go for a wee.

Elderberries are good for your skin,
Figs give you dimples and wrinkles,
Grapes are good with wine,
Haws make you tired and yawn,
While in your bed the Jujubes make you jump for joy.

Kiwi fruit makes you nod and wiggle,
And wiggle and wiggle and wiggle,
Lemons make you roll around which make you
Stand out from the crowd,
Nectarines are little and round.

Oranges are bitter to taste,
Peaches are good for your face,
Quince is good for a race,
Raspberries are full of space.

Strawberries get bits in your face while
Tangerines are small and round,
Watermelons are red and green
With thick skins that make you mean.

But now we have come to an end
With space and taste and lots of things
That in the end will always be
With smiles and glee, wiggles, giggles,
Cringes, bits in your face and lots of taste,
This poem is designed to say that there's
Lots of taste in the world today.

Sam Holland (9)
Staniland Primary School

LET THEM BE

Let the tigers roam free,
Leave their coats for us to see,
Let them be, let them be.

Let the dolphins dive free,
In the crystal clear sea,
Let them be, let them be.

Let the rhinos charge free,
In the wild Serengeti,
Let them be, let them be.

Let the manatees swim free,
The mermaids of the sea,
Let them be, let them be.

Let the elephants graze free,
In the foliage and the tree,
Let them be, let them be.

Let the orangutangs swing free,
High up in the forest canopy,
Let them be, let them be.

Let the pandas climb free,
Up the giant bamboo tree,
Let them be, let them be.

Let the gorillas stride free,
In their hills, so misty,
Let them be, let them be.

Let all the species be free,
The humans hold the key,
To let them be.

Chanelle Swadling (9)
Staniland Primary School

THE PARK

In autumn the park is gold and crispy
The golden animals crawl in the crispy
Rainbowed leaves.

In winter the park is like a
White winter wonderland,
As the animals hibernate
The snow comes down in
A muddled bunch, it covers
The dark green grass.

In spring the park is down
It looks like it's crying
The animals won't come
Out until the rain has stopped
Which they think is dying.

In spring the park is shining because
Now the rain has stopped dying.
The animals come out to
Dance and pray that the rain
Will never come again.

In summer the park
Is shining just like in spring,
The kids are out playing about
While the animals collect
Their food to eat.

Now everyone will
Enjoy themselves
Till the end of the week.

Lesley Stones (10)
Staniland Primary School

MAYBE

It might be a new millennium but nothing's changed.
The bubblegum is still on the pavement and I'm not a millionaire.
But at the end of the tunnel there's light.
Light, shining like light in this unchanging world.
Maybe it'll get better.

Maybe robots will do horrid jobs,
Maybe poverty and war will end.
Maybe in its place there will be happiness.
Maybe we'll all get on.
Maybe the world will become perfect.
Birds will sing and the Earth will be lush.
Maybe global warming and pollution will go away,
Maybe we will all be friends, nations joining one another.
Joy spreading,
Maybe, just maybe.

But until that world comes we shall remain in
The middle of the tunnel.
Never quite reaching the end.
Still the rain falls and people die.
But maybe, just maybe we will reach that world of joy.
Maybe . . .

Fiona Dukalskis (11)
Staniland Primary School

11TH 2000

Today is the year 2000
2000 is a new year
To celebrate the year 2000
We open a can of beer.

Karly Head (8)
Staniland Primary School

THE TRAIN JOURNEY

Yesterday, I went on the train,
It was nothing but a pain.
There was lots of hustle
And plenty of bustle
Before the journey started.

We started down the line,
I found the seat that was mine.
I had a paper to read,
As the train took the lead,
On the journey across the town.

The wheels on the track,
There's no turning back,
With smoke from the funnel,
We went through a tunnel
And everything turned to black.

The train started to slow,
There's nowhere left to go,
It was the end of the line,
So I looked at the sign,
My journey had come to its end.

Sophie Stringer (9)
Staniland Primary School

THE FOUR SEASONS

In winter it is cold and grey
White snow hits your hand and turns into water,
No flowers can be seen.

In spring it is getting hotter and more colourful,
Sunlight hits your hand and tans you
And the flowers start to bloom.

In summer it's really hot and it's as colourful as it gets,
The sun is beaming down
And you can see every flower.

In autumn it gets colder and greyer
Leaves drop off the trees
And flowers die.

Nathan Coupland (11)
Staniland Primary School

MY LAST MEMORIES

As I walked down memory lane,
It all flew back into me,
I tried to fight it
But it caught me
So, here I go, with it inside me.

The radio was on
And me and Mum were sat at the table
Talking,
Then it came on, with Mr Chamberlain,
How the Germans had started the war
We were shocked
And so was our dog Jock.

I was evacuated within four days
And I was in Wales for four years,
When I got home my dog, Jock had been shot
Now it is my turn to go
So have a good life and a very big goodbye.

Emily Laura Jakeman (10)
Staniland Primary School

KIPPER

My dog is called Kipper,
She's black, brown and white,
With long, floppy ears,
Wet nose and bright eyes.

Kipper lies anywhere,
All around the house;
The settee, the chair,
Almost anywhere.
But her favourite
Is my sister's bed
With or without my sister there.

She's five years old,
That's thirty-five in doggy years.
Older than me,
But younger than Dad.

She's soft and furry,
Cuddly and warm.
She's like a pillow when I'm tired
And my head is comfy when I lay near her.

She's my friend all the time,
She doesn't argue or fall out,
She knows I love her
And I know she loves me.

Hallam Williamson (8)
Staniland Primary School

LEO, MY HORSE

I had a horse, his name was Leo,
Riding in the country we would go,
The fields flew past, my hair blew back,
But Leo never faltered in his tracks.

At night his stable welcomed him,
He dreamt of being a champion,
Flying mud, galloping hooves,
Following his tracks in the grooves.

Alix Dodd (8)
Staniland Primary School

AS I WALKED THROUGH THE WOODS

As I walked through the woods,
    I heard wolves tip
    toeing along.
    The flowers were
    tickling my feet

But the sun shines on.
    The sun was setting
    on the horizon.
    It made the sky go
    orange and red.

I heard the mud under my feet.
    The leaves were rushing,
    The trees grow to a tremendous height.

The wind whistled by my face.
    I heard the waterfall
    splashing at the bottom,
    The wood was like
    freezing cold ice.

Water dripped to a puddle at my feet.
    My hair flicked in my face,
    I trembled every step I took.

I want to know what is going on.

Alex Fletcher (10)
Staniland Primary School

QUIET PARK

I love to walk in the park,
especially when it's getting dark,
it's very quiet and you can see
the owls in trees looking down at me!

Alone I think of all my dreams
of days of eating ice-creams!
The street lights are my shiny stars
to guide me through the spooky park.

Rats and mice all scurry round,
to find food people leave around,
it is quite scary on my own
I'll run now so I'll soon be home.

I still think when it's getting dark
the best place is the quiet park.

A place where I can be alone,
before I face my hectic home.

Sam Bedford (9)
Staniland Primary School

THE MYSTICAL UNICORN

U niquely elegant,
N ever noxious,
I mpossible as it seems.
C harming and graceful,
O cculty this creature,
R etreats to the clouds,
    Its wings a flutter.
N ot to be seen again.

Jenna Broome (9)
Staniland Primary School

LET'S GO ARMY GIRLS

She started getting ready
Missing all the people
Killing all the rats as she goes by,
Today has gone well
Getting ready for tomorrow
People are stopping by
Snow is on the ground.
Children sitting on the wall
The parents coming out
They are playing on the sledges
Morning is breaking.
Here is a rat
All bobby and bright,
How do you catch them?
How do you think?
Winning all the money
How do you think!

Emma Reid (11)
Staniland Primary School

THE POKÉMON LEAGUE

Ash, Brock and Misty
Go on a journey,
Up the mountains, across the seas,
They try to get to Pokémon League.
There Pikachu, Charmanda
And Squirtle too.
They have battles and they try to win,
The badges they get on the way
To the Pokémon League.

Nathan Cammack (8)
Staniland Primary School

LAND ARMY GIRLS

Men going off to war
Crying, crying till sunset
Children going away to be safe
Shouting where are you?
It is winter, snow starts
Getting colder and colder
Pulling the plough, getting harder
Men dying quicker and quicker.

Riding horse with the plough
Horse getting tired
Silent track of the day
Getting harder and harder
Day getting darker
Day soon done
Day's done.

Michelle Chamberlain (11)
Staniland Primary School

CHOCOLATES

Chocolates are good for Miss Dawkins,
Especially if all you can hear is munching,
If you like chocolates, here's a little thing that might make you hungry,
Whipple-scrumptious fudge-mallow delight or cavity filling caramels,
Or strawberry juice water pistols, all lickable.

I bet you wish there was a chocolate river,
Just enough for a snake to slither.
Didn't I tell you chocolate is the best thing,
That means I like sugar and milk.

Jade Louisa Teft (8)
Staniland Primary School

MICKEY AND MINNIE

Mickey and Minnie I miss you so,
Mickey and Minnie you lit up my face,
Mickey and Minnie I loved it when you came to the top,
Mickey and Minnie I look in your tank and wonder where you are.
Mickey and Minnie, are you in Heaven safe and sound?
I loved your little face peering at me,
Mickey and Minnie your faces made me laugh when
I cleaned you out,
I miss you so,
I cry and cry when I see your tank,
But I know crying won't bring you back.
Bye Mickey and Minnie goodbye,
I know you're in Heaven, looking down and I'm looking up
To see if you are alright.
Bye bye Mickey,
Bye bye Minnie.

Laura Davenport (10)
Staniland Primary School

THE RAINFOREST

The growing leaves hang over the running streams
Of the dark blue night.
With the running air whistling through the trees.

As the morning sun starts to rise
The animals will get up again
As the brightness of the sun starts
To wake them
The flowers open their petals drinking in the light.

Kerry Ellis (10)
Staniland Primary School

A RAT CATCHER

Talking about home
Writing letters to loved ones
Dreaming of her parents every night she sleeps,
Now she gets up, now the day begins,
She gets to work catching
Rats to save the town.
Then she is going
Down to the fields
She gets the horse
Now she is going to the fields,
She puts the plough on the horse
Then she is going on and on,
It is colder and colder,
Her hands are cold and
Her hands were shaking.

Kasie Watts (10)
Staniland Primary School

THE RUBY-RED CAR

The car is burning down the road,
Its feet make friction along the floor.
He turns his eyes up to full beam,
Then turns them down again.
Every car that comes by gets dazzled because
Of his ruby-red coat,
It shines like the stars at their strongest might.
He just runs out of gas,
He chokes alittle and his engine turns off,
He explores the roads no more.

William Chalmers (10)
Staniland Primary School

THE LAND ARMY WORKERS

At work

They work all day and nearly night,
Digging up and digging down
Backwards, forwards,
All day long
Pulling vegetables here and there
Never resting for a while.

In bed

Sleep at last
Please don't wake me, time for bed
Oh no it's time for work
Up again and dressing quickly
Working quickly as I go
Never stopping till the sun has set.

Vicky Wells (11)
Staniland Primary School

TWICE A DAY

As the rough tough waves hit the sand
And sweeps the shells away
It rocks and rolls the boats out to sea
Dancing them to the cliffs
Then runs away
So all the crabs can be seen
And all the starfish get swept away
Out to sea where they fall to the bottom.
Then going faster and faster again
The sea covers the rock pools
And the crabs once more.

Zoe Stevenson (10)
Staniland Primary School

AS I WALKED THROUGH THE WOODS

As I walked through the woods like a rambler,
I heard the chirping of the chicks,
The flicking of the frog's tongue
The galloping of the heavy horse's hooves.

As I walked through the woods like a pedestrian,
I felt the whistling of the wind,
The rustling of the rustic trees,
The scorching, steaming sun.

As I walked through the woods like a hiker
I saw the famous old oak
The huge wise owl
The bright stars in the sparkling sky.

Justin Coulson (10)
Staniland Primary School

A RAT CATCHER

Here is a rat catcher
Busy and bright,
Why, how do you catch them?
Well how do you think?
By pumping gas down their burrows of course
And blocking the burrows so that none will get out.

So what do you think of your job Mrs Barty?
Well what would you do if my job was yours?
Well I'd chop off their tails
And get some good money,
Well you're very smart 'cause that's what I did,
I chopped off their tails and got one or two pence.

Jamie Hunt (11)
Staniland Primary School

THE RIVER

The river shimmers in the sun,
The tiny pebbles sparkle.

The big splash when rain comes down
The big swish of the waterfall.

The ripple of the water when the wind blows
The flapping of the trees around.

The fish wriggle up stream
The frogs use their big hind legs to swim elegantly.

Winter comes, the river comes to a standstill
Ice descends on the river,
The once beautiful river twirls hard and ugly
Till spring.

Scott Thornley (11)
Staniland Primary School

THE RAINFOREST

The trees are big and round and fat,
I saw a puma, it's like a big cat,
A baby bird is sleeping sweetly,
Its mother made its nest oh so neatly,
I see a poison-arrow frog
And a snake clinging to a log,
A monkey swaying in a tree
Its mother looking fiercely at me,
In the tree, an iguana,
In the lake, a piranha,
On the trees there is rusty bark
In the sky there is a singing lark.

Nicola Snell (10)
Staniland Primary School

AUTUMN TIME

When the leaves are falling off the trees.
When the trees shift from side to side.
When the wind blows fast and hard,
All the birds start to sing and hide.

It is autumn time.

In the morning when you wake up,
The sky is as blue as a sapphire,
Sparkling quite high in the sky.

That is autumn time.

Putting scarves and woolly hats on
And nice warm coats on.

This is autumn time.

Casey Williams (8)
Staniland Primary School

CAN YOU GUESS WHO I AM?

Ghastly guts and lively livers,
Veiny brain and bloody bladders
Can you guess who I am?

Don't judge them by their cover
I work with hundreds of them a day
Rent as many as you want
Can you guess who I am?

I deliver invitations, love letters and all
1st class, 2nd class but no 3rd class,
Can you guess who I am?

Elichia Robinson (10)
Staniland Primary School

CAN YOU GUESS WHAT IT IS?

My nose gets pinched every time I open,
My mouth gets filled with keys,
My eyes get screwed every time I'm loose,
At night I try to get my eyes out to the light switch
And I wonder what life would be like as a school child.

If I have a key in my mouth it looks like my tongue,
I'm a bronze colour but soon I will be
Rusty because of the mitts that touch me,
I am old but I don't know why that changes me.

Have you guessed?

Answer: Door handle.

Kimberley Tyzack (10)
Staniland Primary School

WHICH WAY SHALL I GO NEXT?

The rain drips down shedding its tears
The trees sway waving their arms,
I opened my eyes smelling the fruits,
Clear, fresh and passionate.
I see miniature creatures eating
All different kinds of vegetation.
Next I walk past a pond
I see a poison-arrow frog
Its bright coloration warns me.
An iguana eats a fly
A monkey quickly rushes by
Which way shall I go next?

Carly Clifton (10)
Staniland Primary School

WORLD WAR TWO

W ar has broke out,
O ut goes the land army,
R ight into the countryside,
L ight snow dropping,
D ie if we must.

W orld War Two has started
A nd might get killed,
R egret going in.

T he Germans are almost dead,
W orld War Two has almost finished,
O ver at last.

Paul Barkworth (11)
Staniland Primary School

LEGO

Lego is a fantastic toy,
Made for both girls and boys,
Its range of colours are dark and light,
But mostly they are always bright.

One minute they're big and then they're small
And then there's nothing there at all,
But once again you build your toy
And then you're completely full of joy.

At last my Lego is complete,
It looks so tidy and so neat,
But now it's time to clear and go
And say goodbye to my Lego.

Matthew Lymer (9)
Staniland Primary School

DREAM

As I leave the overt reality,
I slip away, trying to memorise the equation,
It's unstoppable, to resist is futile,
The immortal sandman returns.

As I float around my dream,
I see hills of green and sky of blue,
I see my friends, they see it too,
The dream grows and grows.

A sudden crash on a cloud so white,
I realise that my dream is a nightmare
Only to sight.

Liam Firth (10)
Staniland Primary School

THE CAT

You see it there prowling,
Rats and mice, looking to
Find a tasty snack.

Prowling like a detective,
It finds a helpless rat
Pouncing upon it,
It gets killed, all goes black.

It drags it away to a safe place,
It leaves it there till morning when
To its collection it adds a thrush.
Surely the cat is the prowler champion.

Harley David Cook (10)
Staniland Primary School

NATURE

Nature
Flutter, flutter, butterfly
Your wings flap in the sky,
A sunny day in summertime
So pretty I almost cry.
Flying above the flowers
The trees and hedges too.

Claire Louise Sands (9)
Staniland Primary School

HOMEWORK

Every day I get homework,
But TV's a much more fun time than homework.

Homework isn't as fun as going cycling,
But I must admit it's quite entertaining
Naaa, I think I'll stick with TVing.

Ryan Smith (9)
Staniland Primary School

LIVERPOOL FC

Liverpool is the best,
Robbie Fowler and all the rest!
Goal after goal they score,
This is better than a draw.

Thomas Paul Naylor (8)
Staniland Primary School

GHOST WRITER

I see him write in the air
But my friends say he's never there.

I see him with suspicion on his face
But a pale ghostly figure right in my face.

I see him write in the air again but
All I hear is ghost writer, ghost writer.

Heidi Woods (11)
Staniland Primary School

MEDUSA

M onstrous, beastly, horrible, sister of the Gorgons.
E nding people's lives by turning them into statues.
D readful appalling one glimpse and turned to stone.
U ltimate ugliness, sinister sister.
S nagging snakes in her hair make her monstrous
A nd her life is all over with one look at a mirror.

James Desmond (10)
Staniland Primary School

SNOW

The snow falls on the ground,
The ground is as white as cotton.
We love the snow, say the children,
They rush to the window to have a look,
They dash to get their hats and scarves.

Joseph Andrew (9)
Staniland Primary School

LIKE A WASHING MACHINE

The sea was mighty strong because the
wind blew the sea around and around me.
My fingers were freezing like ice.
I put my fingers in my pocket so they
won't be freezing like ice,
ice made me think about ice-cream.
It made me hungry.

Charlene Atter (10)
Staniland Primary School

CUB CAMP

I've been to cub camp, cub camp, cub camp.
I've been to cub camp, cub camp, cub camp.
We went walking, walking, walking.
We cooked sausages on an open fire.
We went swimming, swimming, swimming.
It was very good, good, good.

Jack Davy (8)
Staniland Primary School

MY RABBIT

My rabbit is ginger with three black stripes
He loves it when I fly my kites
He hates the cold, dark nights
And he never gets into fights.

Craig White (8)
Staniland Primary School

SOUNDLESS SPHINX

S   tanding there in the desert,
P   ointed at all day long,
H   owever, answer her riddle if you can,
I   mpossible to relocate,
N   ow's the time to dash,
X   enophobia is in my heart,
    For I am Egyptian.

Jack Welbourn (9)
Staniland Primary School

MY SEA POEM

The hammering wind made me shiver
As if I was at the North Pole
As if crabs were pinching me
As if I had a needle stuck in me.
The shark was looking at me
Licking his lips.

Luke Revell (10)
Staniland Primary School

A COLD DAY AT THE SEASIDE

The extreme wind made a flag pole swish with the flag,
The sea looked like a powerful tiger, pleading for attention,
My fingers froze but when I put them in my
Pocket they filled with warmth
And my hair blew across my face.

Sarah Edwards (9)
Staniland Primary School

METEORITE

Meteorite, burning bright,
A zooming, flaming ball of light,
A million miles, its massive height,
Quite dazzling, seen by human sight.

Meteorite, travelling far,
Faster than the fastest car,
Against a background of blackish tar,
Dodging every brightening star.

Meteorite, flying low,
Golden particles in tow,
Sparkling like a firework show,
Flying nowhere, it will go.

Meteorite, made of rock,
Flaming in an orange frock,
Flying slowly, now, tick-tock,
Searching for a place to dock.

Meteorite diving down,
An atmospheric, yellow crown,
A planet of unusual brown,
People stare with a puzzled frown.

Ben Edwards (11)
Stickney CE Primary School

SUN

The sun is sitting in the sky
With its great big blue eyes.
The clouds and the sun warm in the skies,
The clouds having fun.

Think of all the wonderful things in the world.
The deep blue sea with its wonderful colours.
The sun and the clouds having fun all day long.
Going on holiday on a vacation for a day.
Making a day better like melting butter.

David Pegg (11)
Stickney CE Primary School

SOLAR

Sun

The sun shines
Day and night
Not always on us
But it's there,
Always shining bright.

The moon glows
From the reflections
Of the sun
Over our country
And then another
One.
Moon.

Planets

The planets turn
Just hovers around
Spinning in
The solar system,
Not making a sound.

Jake Gosling (11)
Stickney CE Primary School

THE UNIVERSE

We are in space
Floating, watching and discovering
The planets are multicolours
As we fly gently past them.

The stars are shiny and bright
As they glisten and sparkle in black space.
We see the Milky Way
And we run slowly across it.

Astronauts wave at us
In their shuttle crafts
Comets whiz fastly by
Past the sun, moon and Earth.

The Universe is gigantic
And man will never conquer it,
That's why
The Universe is a big dark secret.

Charmaine Currie (11)
Stickney CE Primary School

UP, UP AND AWAY

The aeroplane
I'm a plane,
As red as a rose,
I fly through the cloud,
As fast as an arrow.

I'm a plane,
Looking down at the land,
I see a big brass band
With a conductor waving his hand.

I'm a plane,
Flying over the roofs, up, up and away,
Around the world in one day,
London, New York and Italy too,
I'll be glad to get home and see you.

I'm a plane,
About to land,
Bump! Crash! Bang!
I'm glad to be on solid land.

Andrew Wooding (11)
Stickney CE Primary School

A SPACESHIP

A spaceship in the sky,
Who knows what's inside,
A spaceship in the sky, will it fly?
Who's inside?

Swooping past Mars,
There's something inside,
Flying by the stars,
Who's inside?

Hurtling past Saturn,
There's something green inside,
The spaceship's making patterns,
Who's inside?

The spaceship's landed,
An alien has come out,
The alien is empty handed,
Now I know who's inside.

Francesca Cash (10)
Stickney CE Primary School

ON TOP OF THE WORLD

A kite flying high
In the sunny cloudless sky
With a string attached to the end
In case it should intend
To fly away high
And leave the world behind
Sample life living
On top of the world.

Break through the clouds
Hear the different sounds
See the unusual sights
On this adventurous flight
Look down below
See the world go
It's a totally different life
Living on top of the world.

Rebecca Hall (11)
Stickney CE Primary School

A LEAF

I'm a leaf
I'm green and free
I used to live with my family
On an oak tree.

I sat on a twig
Until the wind blew me away
So now I spend my time
Fluttering around all day.

I twirl and swirl
I float around in the sky
No one can catch me
Because I'm flying so high.

The day is turning
Into night
But I will keep
Floating until
I'm out of sight.

Amy Barker (10)
Stickney CE Primary School

KITE

The sky is so blue,
No clouds to be seen,
What's that? What's this?
A kite is on the scene.

Orange and blue,
Glistening against the sun,
Gliding swiftly,
The kite is having so much fun.

I close my eyes
And dream it is me,
I'm that kite in the sky,
Flying so free.

I dream about all the things,
That I would see high above,
I opened my eyes to find,
My beloved kite had gone.

Rachael Burman (11)
Stickney CE Primary School

KITE'S LIFE

I'm a kite on the ground,
Throw me I will fly.
I'll go . . . round your head,
High as a house,
Just let me go mad.

I'm a kite in the air,
Soaring through the sky.
But the winds drop
When I'm over a tree.
I fall and get stuck.

I'm a kite in a tree
A child cries for me.
I'm so sad I fall out
And I land in the child's hands.

Hooray I'm alive, I'm free!
Same time, same place next week.

Sophie Marston (11)
Stickney CE Primary School

LEAF

Flying so high, leaving the tree
Whimpering and scared,
No one knows what I feel to be free,
Finally, at last.

To be free was my dream,
But suddenly
There I was laying, crying for help,
But no one came.

Speaking my last words, I say farewell
Sad to say goodbye,
For someone will replace.

Farewell my job is done,
Now to go and leave in peace,
For, I will be back,
So I say farewell.

Gary Gosling (11)
Stickney CE Primary School

KITE

I am a kite so straight and tall
When I fly through the air
I don't care at all.
I buzz here and there like a bumblebee,
Flying at heights doesn't matter to me
Because people who watch all wish they were me.

I am a kite so cool and sleek
Thrown in the air and swept off my feet
It doesn't really bother me,
I'm glad I'm a kite, it's good to be me.

Flying over the trees that stand so tall,
Compared to me so sleek and small
And when I'm pulled down to the ground
I really feel quite safe and sound.

Keilan Gilbert (11)
Stickney CE Primary School

I Am A Leaf

I am a little leaf
With little shiny teeth
They glitter all day
And glitter all night
But nobody has a fright.

I am a leaf
Got nowhere to go
All I do is just float like a bird.

I am a leaf
With big shiny underpants
They just shine all day
And shine all night and everyone
Has a smelly night.

Ben Willis (11)
Stickney CE Primary School

Roller-Coaster

A roller-coaster zoom, zoom round, upside down, slow, fast,
A scream as loud as a football ground cheer but louder.
25 people on the roller-coaster, shaking teeth banging together,
One man controlling it, '50p please for a ride, thank you.'
The controller shifts on the roller-coaster click, zoom, zoom,
Off it goes.
The controller checking everyone's in safe,
Last ride, the millions of people line up for a ride
Only 25 allowed,
People walk away
The controller only says, 'Come back tomorrow.'

Mark Veall (10)
Stickney CE Primary School

AN AEROPLANE

If I were an aeroplane I would . . .

Fly around the sky,
Acting stunts with care,
Up, up, high,
Blazing through the air.

In the clouds amazing all the people
360 degrees around the village steeple.

I could . . .

Take people away to other places
Filling airport timetable spaces.

To be a plane would be great for a day
But I'd prefer to be a boy and play!

Harry Richards (10)
Stickney CE Primary School

A BIRD

I am a bird in the air,
Flying here, there and everywhere,
I can see for miles around,
Eating insects off the ground,
Dragonflies, small grasshoppers,
That is what is on a bird's mind,
Yum yum I wish you could join me.

Nicola Whiteley (10)
Stickney CE Primary School

THE SUN AND THE MOON

I am the sun, a big shiny sun
Surrounded by clouds
With nothing to do
Except shine, shine, shine.

I stay up in the air
With the sky and the clouds
I am stuck up here all by myself
Moon will you be my friend?

I am the moon, I'm also bright
You can't see me in the day
Only in the dark of the night
Yes I will be your friend.

Marc Nisbet (11)
Stickney CE Primary School

ROLLER-COASTER HORRORS

The roller-coaster horrors are coming back to town.
The roller-coaster horrors are making people frown.
There's a swerve and there's a twist.
Then the roller-coaster is in the mist.

Then you can see it . . .
Going up, up and away.
Round a hoop and into a loop.
It really is worse than a bowl of soup.

Then it gets slower and lower,
Then bang it stops.
Tang the lights flicker
And people are getting sicker.

Elizabeth Challis (10)
Stickney CE Primary School

UP, UP AND AWAY

The clouds go round and round
The birds wings go flap, flap, flap,
The clouds go bang, bang
The birds fly away,

The sun is bright,
The moon is dull,
The sun is orange,
The sky is blue.

The wind blows
The rain comes down,
The wind is fast and
The rain is slow
And a stream flows.

Mark Bogg (10)
Stickney CE Primary School

WHAT IS . . . THE SUN?

The sun is an orange marble
Rolling outside Earth.

It's an orange volleyball
Bouncing up and down.

It's a gold earring stud
That's piercing the sky.

It's a golden eye
Watching out to sea.

It's a yellow roundabout
Being dizzy every day.

Clare Louise Wood (10)
Swineshead St Mary's Primary School

PAINTBOX MUSIC

If I could write violet music
It would be friendly and light music
It would be lovely and happy music
It would be as happy as ever.

If I could write yellow music
It would be bright and jolly music
It would be big and young music
It would be spring music.

If I could write romantic music
It would be silent and slow music
It would be kissing music
It would be love music.

If I could write me music
It would be spicy and scary music
It would be spider music
It would be me music.

Jane Webster (11)
Swineshead St Mary's Primary School

PAINTBOX MUSIC

If I could write white music
It would be calm and sleepy music
It would be plain and lazy music
It would be misty music.

If I could write orange music
It would be bright and tasty
It would be warm and sticking music
It would be sweet music.

If I could write me music
It would be quiet and loud music
It would be happy and sad music
It would be seasonal music.

Jacky Nunn (10)
Swineshead St Mary's Primary School

THE PEOPLE OF NARZ

H ello to all the creatures,
O n Earth, Neptune and Mars,
W e're all alike yet different,

W hen it comes to Narz.
E verybody has to talk

A varied talk indeed:
'R ruubbeededubeedeedo,'
E merges at great speed.

A nd when they walk, they stride great
L engths in very little time,
L ilting songs do take them through a

D ay of heavy rhyme.
I f anybody asks them:
'F riend, what doth make ye sing?'
'F or pleasure,' is their stout response
'E xcitement and such things'
'R ruubbeededubeedeedo,'
E xclaim the Men from Narz
N ever ever thinking
T hat they live in my jam jars.

James McDonald (11)
Swineshead St Mary's Primary School

PAINTBOX MUSIC

If I could write gold music
It would be precious and special music
It would be bright and glamorous music
It would be sun music.

If I could write black music
It would be spooky and dark music
It would be dull and thunderous music
It would be ghost music.

If I could write white music
It would be cloudy and soft music
It would be calm and misty music
It would be fresh music.

If I could write me music
It would be happy and sad music
It would be soft and hard music
It would be me music!

Victoria Joy Mayhem (11)
Swineshead St Mary's Primary School

GOLDEN

A golden lion in a zoo
Shakes his mane, just for you,
People laying on golden hay
They lay on hay all the day.
Taste of the golden honey
Fills my purse with golden money.
My dog is wearing a necklace gold
Makes me shiver, I am so cold.

Kurt Matthew Scott (8)
Westmere Community Primary School

GOLDEN

Golden glistening sands of time
Locked in a golden box of mine
Golden locks of golden hair
A golden child with a golden stare
A golden sun in a golden sky
A twinkle in my golden eye
A sunshine ray of golden light
A golden ghost in the night
Golden rings upon my finger
Golden spirits tend to linger
Golden is the golden colour
A ghost is the golden horror
A golden man wants to stay
Golden instruments will they play?
Golden ducks in a stream
The golden clouds by the golden sun
The animals play with golden sun.

Kirsty Hennessey (9)
Westmere Community Primary School

IF THINGS GREW DOWN

If things grew down instead of up,
A dog would turn into a pup,
A bee would turn into a fly,
A child would turn into a baby and cry.
If a girl would turn into a boy,
A boy would turn into a toy.
Big would turn into something small
And small would turn into nothing at all.

Natasha Remmig (9)
Westmere Community Primary School

GOLDEN

Golden sunshine
Brightens the sky
Flashes of golden
My oh my.

Golden daffodils
Flowing in the breeze
Golden fruit on
Golden trees.

Golden saxophone
Playing notes,
Floating softly
Flows golden boats.

Golden hair
Flows in the sun
Blows in the wind
But still having fun.

My best friend
Saying golden speech
Laying, sunbathing
On the golden beach.

Frankie Jackson (9)
Westmere Community Primary School

GOLDEN

Rising brightly, the golden sun
Wakes the day with special fun,
She strolls the sky in a golden ray
Picking the golden daffodils on her way.
Jumping and leaping goldfish play

Golden sand on which to lay.
Golden apples and golden leaves
Hanging ripe and juicy on golden trees
The golden sun will keep them warm
Just like the golden corn.

Lauren Elizabeth Alford (9)
Westmere Community Primary School

GOLDEN

Rising brightly, the golden sun
Wakes the day with special sun
She strolls the sky in a golden ray
Picking the golden, daffodils on her way.
Jumping and leaping the goldfish play
Golden sand on which to lay
Golden apples and golden leaves
Handing ripe and juicy on golden trees
She eats golden pears
And flowers in her golden hair.

Sinead Mackman (9)
Westmere Community Primary School

IF THINGS GREW DOWN

If things grew down instead of up
A dog would grow into a pup,
A cat would grow into a kitten,
Your sweater would grow into a mitten.
A cow would grow into a calf
And a whole would grow into a half,
Big would grow into something small
And small would grow into nothing at all.

Dudley Long & Jenna Duncan (9)
Westmere Community Primary School

SWIM WITH ME TO MY TROPICAL ISLAND

Swim with me to my tropical island
Come paddle aboard the sea
Come relax yourself in warm water
Try the coconuts taste with me.

Come make shapes in the sand
Sit right beside the smooth trees
Let's all look at the toucans
And see the floating leaves.

Come with me to my tropical island
Come with me please come with me.

Todd Aldhous (9)
Westmere Community Primary School

SWIM WITH ME TO MY TROPICAL ISLAND

Swim with me to my tropical island
Come on just swim with me
Come and see my sparkling lagoon
Oh please come and see.

Oh you can kiss my toucans
And swim in the sea
If you don't want to swim alone
I will swim with you, you'll see.

Oh please come to my tropical island
Please come please.

Stephanie Callaby (9)
Westmere Community Primary School

SWIM WITH ME TO MY TROPICAL ISLAND!

Come and swim with me just come and swim
Come and see my sparkling lagoon
And you come with me on my jet ski
Come and see the lovely moon.

Come and see my new jet ski
It can go as fast as the day
It will sparkle in the moonlight
And you can lay in the hay.

Come and swim with me just come and swim
With me to my tropical island.

Connor Young (9)
Westmere Community Primary School

GOLDEN

Golden keys open golden locks,
People wearing golden socks,
Golden cattle in a golden barn,
Rustling in the golden farm.

Golden fish in a golden stream,
Golden top with a golden seam,
Golden sun over golden hay,
Golden girl in golden play.

Goldfish in a goldfish play,
As the sun goes down at the end of the day.

Stacey Smalley (8)
Westmere Community Primary School

ON A BLUE DAY

On a blue day
When the brown heat
Scorches the grass
And stings my legs with sweat.

I go running like a fool
Up the hill towards the trees
And my heart beats loudly
Like a kettle boiling dry.

I need a bucket the size of the sky
Filled with cool, cascading water.

An evening
The cool air rubs my back
I listen to the bees
Working for their honey.

The sunset pours light
Over my head like a waterfall.

Jade Robinson (9)
Westmere Community Primary School

IF THINGS GREW DOWN

If things grew down instead of up,
A saucer would grow into a cup!
The sun would grow into a ball,
A chair would grow into a stool!
A dress would grow into a skirt,
A skirt would grow into a shirt!
Big would grow into something small
And small would grow into nothing at all.

Kate Stratton (9)
Westmere Community Primary School

GOLDEN

Awakes the golden sun
He shines brightly in the sky
Children dancing with great fun
As it grows higher in golden day.

As it shines upon the golden hay
Coming down upon the day.
The golden lion in the zoo
Swings his mane just for you.

It shines on the golden hay
And the sun won't go down until
The strike of dusk
Ends the day.

Sam Cooper (9)
Westmere Community Primary School

SWIM WITH ME TO MY TROPICAL ISLAND

Swim with me to my tropical island
Come and have a swim with me
Come and have some tea
Come and climb my tree.

You can play in the sand
And look at land
You can eat mangoes
You can throw sand.

Swim with me to my tropical island
Swim with me!

Arron Drew (9)
Westmere Community Primary School

RIVERS

Rivers swaying like the wind, swish, swash,
Swish, swash.
Rivers flowing like the sea making loud noises.
Rivers floating like a fish in a fish tank.
Rivers are rough like a boxing match.
Rivers are tough like the wind.
Rivers are frothy like a bath.
Rivers are smooth as a rug.
Rivers swirl like a whirlpool.

Hannah Boyes (7)
Wrangle Primary School

RIVERS

Rivers follow behind the fish.
Rivers sway from side to side.
Rivers flow along the bank.
Rivers whistling like the wind.
Rivers float back and forth.
Rivers are cold just like ice that cools you
Down day and night.

Becky Gostelow (8)
Wrangle Primary School

THE RIVER

Where does the river start?
Does the splashing river start in the mountain
Or does it start in the sea?
I don't quite know where the splashing river starts
Because I haven't quite been to see!

I stood at the side of the deep blue stream,
I saw a waterfall and went to listen,
When all I could hear was the sea getting near
Going splish, splash, splish, splash.

Skye Cotter (10)
Wrangle Primary School

SPRING

Spring is wonderful when the flowers start
to blossom,
Spring is colour all around.
Spring is pretty, meek and mild,
Spring is peaceful, hardly making a sound.
Spring is lovely,
Spring is warm,
Spring comes once a year when everything is
born.

Leon Bailey (9)
Wrangle Primary School

RIVERS

Rivers crushing stones all around,
Rivers crashing along the ground,
Rivers bashing while passing by,
Rivers bubbling around the sea,
Rivers swirling with joy and glee,
Rivers rushing and then you find,
Stones and fish, many a kind.

George Kime (8)
Wrangle Primary School

THE HORSEMAN

Clip, clop go the horse's feet,
Trotting through the fallen leaves.
The clouds are coming closer,
As the nights are drawing in.
When the horse goes in its stable,
And as the horseman closes the stable door,
He hears a clap of thunder.
The autumn wind blows,
And the leaves are swept around his feet.
He heads inside clutching his coat
While feeling the temperature drop.
When he gets inside he will light a fire,
Then eventually go to bed.
In the morning when he wakes up
He will go through to start another day.

Rianna Hooke (11)
Wrangle Primary School

SPRING

Blossom on the treetops
I love little chocolate drops
Little white clouds passing by
Spring has new treetops in the blue sky
Small white and yellow daisies
Little buzzing bees going crazy,
Daffodils smiling,
Baby lambs lying,
And they sing, sing, sing
While they're getting ready for spring, spring,
Spring!

Victoria Pinchbeck (9)
Wrangle Primary School

RIVER COURSE

What makes the boggy river source?
The falling rain, of course.
Oh where does the deep river start?
In the high hills of Wales, of course.
Oh how does the big, big river get bigger?
By eroding rocks and gravel, of course.
Oh why do the falling waterfalls start?
Because the rushing river can't erode the hard, hard rock.
Oh where do the soft sands come from?
From the river bottom of course.
Oh where does a trickling tributary go?
It's one little stream joining the river, of course.
What are the curves of the river?
Meanders, of course.
Oh where is the flood valley?
In the middle course, of course.
Oh why does the large, flowing and deep river flow so
                        steadily near the deep, deep sea?
Because it's sad and its long journey's over.

George Miller (11)
Wrangle Primary School

SPRING

Yippee, it's spring today, the day when children sing
Trees blossom, leaves are green
Bees are buzzing on the fragrant flowers.
Birds are singing on the blooming trees
Beautiful butterflies fluttering in the breeze
Silky petals soft as a baby's face to the touch
Sunny skies with creamy clouds on top of a
                        blueberry ice-cream.

Emma Garner (8)
Wrangle Primary School

THE MIST POEM

The mist's freezing, blistering,
Cold air twists and turns through the air
It freezes to trees
dock leaves, grass and dandelions.
The wet puddles that have been made by rain
are nearly frozen because of the mist and its cold air.
The people are walking down the street
with woolly hats and woolly gloves
and dogs wear little coats because
of the mysterious mist.
In the woods the pine needles, sticks and
the woodland grasses are all covered
in the cold air's mist.
In the mountains the tall mountains, rocks
and small mountains
are slippery and icy from the cold air's mist.
Now slowly and surely the sun rises
and the mist slowly and surely
vanishes into thin air.

Daniel Bee (9)
Wrangle Primary School

RIVERS

Rivers flow up and down.
Rivers go smoothly across the bank.
Rivers whistle like a bird.
Rivers flow rough and smooth.
Rivers follow each other like us.
Rivers crash into the rocks.

Chelsea Howes (8)
Wrangle Primary School

RIVERS

Rivers are see-through,
Clear and bright,
Rivers sparkle,
Very light,
Rivers ripple,
Rivers flow,
They can be slow
As fast as snow,
Rivers froth,
Like bubble bath.
Rivers wave,
Up and down.
Rivers bend,
Like a snake,
Twisting and turning like the number eight.

James Arnold (9)
Wrangle Primary School

RIVERS

Rivers flow for ever and ever,
But rivers aren't very clever.
Rivers are just as fast as a car,
But they don't go as far.
Rivers crash into the side,
As they glide like skates on ice.
Rivers make lots of sounds,
And love to bound and bound around.
Rivers flow for ever and ever,
But rivers aren't very clever.

Leigh Overton (9)
Wrangle Primary School

BUBBLES

Red bubbles, green bubbles,
Floating in the sink,
Yellow bubbles, purple bubbles,
Making me blink.

Blue bubbles, pink bubbles,
Going round and round.
Bubbles going up and up,
Then bursting to the ground.

Bubbles, bubbles everywhere
For everyone to see
Clap my hands, 1, 2, 3,
Then I start to scream.

Sarah Gostelow (10)
Wrangle Primary School

RIVERS

Rivers are see-through
    Clear and bright
Rivers are bendy
    Like a water slide
Rivers are cold
    Like an ice-cube
Rivers are bubbling
    Like bubble foam in a bath
Rivers are drippy
    Dripping down my leg
Rivers are never-ending
    Flowing through the riverbed.

Thomas Brooks (8)
Wrangle Primary School

SPRING

Leaves falling on the ground
While my little sister's turning round
Fresh blossom in the air
While blowing through my golden hair
Daffodils blowing, all day long
While buzzing bees are being lazy
Baby lambs lying down
Ready for spring to jump around.

Charlotte Burton (8)
Wrangle Primary School

THE CHAMELEON

The ever changing camouflaged chameleon
Moves steadily and slowly like an old man
Waddling towards a branch.
Its flexible eyes ever looking round for predators.
And his long tongue with the bugs *zap*
They never know what hits them.

Jarron Marshall (9)
Fleetwood Lane CP School

HAPPINESS

Happiness is light purple
Happiness tastes like ice-cream running down your throat,
Happiness feels soft and smooth,
Happiness smells sweeter than all the flowers in the world.
Happiness sounds like bird song filling the air.

Victoria Bray Whitworth (10)
Fleetwood Lane CP School

OUTER SPACE

Outer space is brilliant
With the sun, a moon and a star,
Some of space is near
And some of it's afar.

You can see the planets,
Mercury, Venus and Mars.
And when you look more closely
You can see the stars.

Everything in space
Is called the Universe
And when I say everything
That includes the Earth.

Jupiter and Saturn are part
Of the Universe as well.
Uranus and Neptune have very strong winds,
But they're hard to tell.

Pluto's small and rocky,
Plus it's far away,
Outer space is brilliant
To explore another day.

Jonathan Birchall (8)
Fleetwood Lane CP School

THE WATER FIGHT

I loaded my gun
Ready to have fun
I hid behind a wall
That was pretty tall.
I shot my friend
And reloaded again.

The enemy came
And I shot him again.
My gun was empty, so I had to take the risk,
Of going to the tap, I had to run very fast.
When he came I ran out of his line of fire,
But got shot and landed in the mire.

Jeremy Ely (9)
Fleetwood Lane CP School

WONDERING ABOUT SPACE

While I'm counting stars,
I'm wondering if aliens live on Mars?

Pluto is very small but
Jupiter is the biggest of them all.

I wonder if Planet Zog
Is a bit of tape, is it a different shape?

Or in the spaceship,
The astronauts are playing sports?

The astronauts run in the bar
Like a shooting star.

I wonder what it's like being
A star and be very far
And be very high in the sky?

I wonder what it's like being an
Astronaut, do you go to the airport?
And go in a spaceship and go zooming
Off like a felt tip.

Beth Davis (9)
Fleetwood Lane CP School

A LIGHT THAT IS DARK

A heart full of war
A baby full of power
A spotless ladybird
A mouse-sized tower

A silent roar
A bare cluttered floor
A colourful whiteness
An exciting bore

A four-cornered circle
A loser that won
An unlit star
A blackout lined sun

A kind-hearted thief
A flat and straight curl
A dry patch of river
A black and grey pearl

Stephanie Wilkinson (11)
Fleetwood Lane CP School

PUDDINGS

I like ice-cream, cold and sweet
I like cake, soft and fruity
I like to see, jelly wobble on a plate
I like fruit in a tin
I like bananas mixed with custard,
Puddings, puddings are very nice
Give me pudding all day and night
But best of all it has to be
Ice-cream!

Daniel Godfrey (9)
Fleetwood Lane CP School

A FISTFUL OF PACIFISTS

A nut of apples
A meeting of pears
A bucket of rain
A count-up of hairs

A rumble of rockets
A cluster of sharks
A mouthful of silence
A quietness of sparks

A shout of football
A whisper of the crowds
A downfall of rain
A referee's decision allowed

A strike of lightning
A sin box of sons
A survivor of strike
A basketful of buns.

George Miller (10)
Fleetwood Lane CP School

THE BIRD

Wood-pecker
Worm-snatcher
Nest-sitter
Bird-watcher
Loud-singer
Branch-sitter
Long-flyer

Samuel Collins (10)
Fleetwood Lane CP School

SNOWBOARDING

The air is cold
The sky is blue
The slope was steep
And down I flew.

I went down a half-pipe
There was lots of snow
I saw my friends
And they too had a go.

The air was biting
The sky was full of snow
Give me a push
And down I go.

I went on the board park
There was a big jump
I fell off my snowboard
And landed with a thump.

Edward Ashton (8)
Fleetwood Lane CP School

THE HORSE

Good racer
Horse rider
Grass eater
Fast runner
Big winner
Big horse
Swift runner.

Desmond Riley (11)
Fleetwood Lane CP School

WHO AM I?

Sea hunter
Night haunter

Big splasher
Teeth snatcher

Fish killer
Majestic swisher

Sudden sinker
Skin tickler

Sharp jaws
With two rows

      A catalogue to make
             me a
                 shark.

Rishul Padhiar (11)
Fleetwood Lane CP School

LILLY ATE

Lilly ate cake
Lilly ate jelly
Lilly went to bed
With a pain in her belly.
Don't be mistaken
Don't be misled
For all that
She had was
A pain in her head.

Brett Britton (10)
Fleetwood Lane CP School

MY PET

My pet is cuddly
But naughty
My pet is good
But bad
My pet is fat
But thin
My pet is nice
But fierce
My pet is clever
But silly
My pet is big
But small
My pet is walking
But running
My pet is fast
But slow.

Charlie Rose (8)
Fleetwood Lane CP School

OWL

Mouse-hunter
Night-flyer
Day-sleeper
Chick-beater
Hooting-hunter
Field-scavenger
Swift-sweeper
Fast-flyer
Picky-pecker.

Mark Frost (11)
Fleetwood Lane CP School

JAPONICA FIVE

A water leaker,
A groaning creeker
A quiet slinker
A 30's clinker
A huge large gaffrig
All damp and humid
Live rough and ready
Your head feels heavy
You're sick and queasy
Cause the wind's breezy
Go howl on the holy yard,
Watch out for that mallard
The wind on the sail
Behind the ropes trail.
A catalogue to make me
A yacht.

Robin Wilson (10)
Fleetwood Lane CP School

KINGFISHER

Fish-eater
Swift-swooper
Water-glider
Fish-watcher
Treetop-watcher
Fish-stalker
Lake-fighter
Fish-catcher
Kingfisher.

James Moore (11)
Fleetwood Lane CP School

THE MONSTER

Monster, monster,
What a sight
Monster, monster,
Want a bite?
Monster, monster,
What a fright.

Monster, monster,
In the night
Monster, monster,
You are so smelly,
Monster, monster,
You are as big as a nelly,
Monster, monster,
What a fright!

Matthew Shire (8)
Fleetwood Lane CP School

KID

Leaf kicker
Snowball flicker
Summer paddler
Spring saddler
Ice skimmer
Lake-swimmer
Woolly jumper
Summer camper.

Lots of energy to make me a
k i d.

Josephine Scully (11)
Fleetwood Lane CP School

SPACE RACE

The race is loud
The race is rough
The race is tough
You get bumped
You get hurt and smashed.

I walloped someone
Up the back of the shuttle
I jumped over the moon
He jumped over me
Everybody took the lead
I sped off.

I caught up second
Place and won the race!

Elliott Harris (9)
Fleetwood Lane CP School

TIGER

Meat-eater
Giant-heater
Night-patroller
Animal-controller
Midnight-runner
Dangerous-stunner
Ground-croucher
Animal-counter
Stone-kicker
Meat-licker.

Edward Burton (10)
Fleetwood Lane CP School

THE WEATHER

A snow sender
A wind wailer

A hail hailer
A tide breaker

A ship tipper
A hurricane swirler

A building toppler
A sun burner

A mysterious master.

All this adds up to the
Weather.

Jack Glauser (10)
Fleetwood Lane CP School

TIGER

A deep napper,
A tooth snapper
A prey spotter
A swift trotter
A food seeker
A eye peeker
A razor claw
A huge jaw
A furry coat
A giant throat.

Davy Shepherd (10)
Fleetwood Lane CP School

FIRE, FIRE

Fire's blazing like the sun
A wild beast scanning the land
Biting everything he sees
Roaring underneath the trees.

Biting, stretching
Over what all can be seen
Blazing to the bushes
Stretching over the world so big.

The fire is still hungry
A wild beast or not
It has to be full up soon
Alas it has died down
Eaten animals out of house and home.

Melissa Rae Bradley (9)
Fleetwood Lane CP School

THE DOG

Kennel-sleeper
Floor-sweeper
Pond-fisher
Dish-licker
Absolute-stunner
Fast-runner
Rabbit-racer
Mouse-taster
Plant-lifter
Garden-shifter.

George Spencer (10)
Fleetwood Lane CP School

SPORT, SPORT, SPORT

Bat and ball,
Wicket in place,
England lose,
What a disgrace.

Pot the white,
Foul shot played,
Championship hopes,
Begin to fade.

Placed on the spot,
Goalie set,
Striker steps us,
In the net.

Daniel Stanton (11)
Fleetwood Lane CP School

THE DOG

Bowl-licker
House-sleeper
Water-drinker
Ball-player
Loud-barker
Tail-wagger
Robber-catcher
Cat-chaser
Biscuit-eater
Tree-climber
Mole-catcher.

David Almey (10)
Fleetwood Lane CP School

ZEBRA

A horse with black and white stripes
And camouflage itself.

This particular animal is very fast
When being attacked and is a very
Popular zoo animal.

It's a wild cats favourite food.

It's as fast as a racing car and
A very popular horse.

It eats grassy things and sounds like a donkey.

This horse lives in a hot country
It lives mostly in Africa.

Laura Newson (9)
Fleetwood Lane CP School

THE DOG

Basket-hogger
Water-lapper
Fire-heater
Bone-eater
Friendly-player
Ball-player
Stick-catcher
Loud-barker
Children-fusser
Bedroom-sleeper
Mad-runner.

Alex West (10)
Fleetwood Lane CP School

WHY SPACE?

Why is the fireball called the sun?
Why has Saturn got rings why not the moon?
Why is Venus called Venus?
And why is the Earth chosen to have living things?

Why does a black hole suck in not out?
Why do stars shine so bright?
Why has the moon got craters?
And why can I see them at night?

Why is Jupiter the largest planet?
Why do spacemen have space suits?
Why does the countdown go 3, 2, 1, not 1, 2, 3?
And why is Venus the hottest planet not Mercury?

Christopher Neve (9)
Fleetwood Lane CP School

A NIGHT-BARKER

A night-barker
A nosy-parker
A hand-licker
A football-kicker
A foot-heater
A keen-eater
A super-runner
A kind hearted-stunner
A cat-chaser
A whizzing past-racer
A catalogue to make me a dog.

Libby Sanderson (10)
Fleetwood Lane CP School

My Best Friend

My best friend is funny
But serious
My best friend is tall
But small.
My best friend is not very thin
But not very fat.
My best friend is blonde
Not brown.
My best friend has green eyes
Not blue.
My best friend is kind
But only sometimes rude.
I like my best friend anyway.

Sarah Harvey (8)
Fleetwood Lane CP School

Motor Cross

Super cross is good,
Super cross is bad,
But I like it when
You fly down the track.
'This is good'
I say as I zoom
Down the track.
Well, but better
Than that is as
You fly over
The jumps.

Luke Orrey (8)
Fleetwood Lane CP School

LITTLE JACK SPRAT

Little Jack Sprat
Once had a pig,
It was not very little,
Nor yet very big,
It was not very lean,
It was not very fat -
It's a good pig to grunt,
Said little Jack Sprat
Poor little Jack with the dreaded flu,
What will little Jack do?
Oink, oink said little Jack's pig,
I know what to do,
If you have the flu.

Aimie Seth (8)
Fleetwood Lane CP School

THE LION

A lion is rough, a lion is tough,
He wandered through the grasses and leaves.
The lion loves to eat
He would beat someone for the meat
He runs out looking for the food
When he can't, he gets in a mood.
When he can't catch the food.
The lion is mad, the lion is bad,
The lion is large, the lion's going to charge
The lions favourite meal is deer,
So the deer is in fear.

Daniel Taylor (10)
Fleetwood Lane CP School

DUCKS

A bread snatched,
A fish catcher.

A duck and diver
A great survivor.

A pond lover,
A caring mother.

A brood carer,
A duckling sharer.

A catalogue to make me a
Duck!

Samantha Ellis (10)
Fleetwood Lane CP School

DOG

Loud-bark
Sharp-claws
Cuddly-toys
Smelly-breath
Floppy-ears
Fast-runner
Tree-scratcher
Shoe-eater
Cat-chaser
High-jumper
Gate-hurdler
Hand-licker.

Thomas Godfrey (10)
Fleetwood Lane CP School

THE WEATHER

A snowstorm,
A rainy morning.

A sunny summer,
A wind hammer.

A winter so cold,
A spring so bold.

A wave wrinkler,
A boat sinker.

A cloudy day,
Scattered hay.

Sally Harrison (10)
Fleetwood Lane CP School

A CAT

Tree-scratcher
Ball-snatcher
Night-creeper
Fish-eater
Milk-lapper
Paw-tapper
Basket-sleeper
Fire-heater
Loud-hisser
Wet-kisser

A catalogue to make me a cat.

Emma Burnett (10)
Fleetwood Lane CP School

MIRACLE MAN

My dad's a miracle man
He's big, strong and brave
He will ride the highest roller-coaster
And come down still as brave.

My dad's a miracle man
He can do whatever he wants
He could travel to the stars
And then go off to Mars.

My dad's a miracle man
He'll jump off a dam
The only problem is he doesn't like ham.

Joshua Turner (9)
Fleetwood Lane CP School

THE DOME

The year 2000 has come at last
It's time to put the sadness
And tears in the past.
The future holds many surprises
Who knows what they will be.
We'll just have wait and see
Maybe I'll win the lottery.

If I do that is great
Who knows what you can
Do with that amount of money.
Maybe a Porsche that goes very fast,
As we go past the M1 road.

Andrew John Forman (8)
Fleetwood Lane CP School

WINNING GOAL

W   imbledon
I   ncredible goal
N   aughty Nottingham
N   aughty but nice Norwich
I   nvisable Preston
N   ewcastle magpies, flying high
G   oalies diving mad.

G   oals come crazy
O   ffensive referee
A   nonymous Luton
L   eague champions again.

Chris Harris (11)
Fleetwood Lane CP School

THE SEA

The sea is blue
The sea is clean
Some of the animals can be mean
The sea can be nice
The sea can be bad
It is nice for a little lad
The sea is long
The sea is big
In the sea it is hard to dig
The sea is refreshing
The sea is cool
It is like a giant swimming pool.

Daniel Coleman (10)
Fleetwood Lane CP School

MY CATS

My cat's bad
your
cat's good

My cat's silly
your
cat's good

My cat's brown
your
cat's grey

My cat's small
your
cat's big

My cat's funny
your
cat's not

My cat's quick
your
cat's slow

My cat's a boy
your
cat's a girl.

April Harris (9)
Fleetwood Lane CP School